# Sir Alfred Haslam

## Marine Refrigeration Pioneer
## Derby

## Geoff Sadler and Joan D'Arcy

Sir Alfred Seale Haslam, 1844-1927 [National Portrait Gallery]

Sir Alfred Seale Haslam

ISBN 978 0 86071 849 9

A Commissioned Publication Printed by

MOORLEYS
Print, Design & Publishing
info@moorleys.co.uk • www.moorleys.co.uk

# Acknowledgements

Acknowledgments go to all the people who have helped and advised in various ways in producing this book.

First of all, thanks to Alison Haslam, great granddaughter of William Gilbert Haslam. He was Sir Alfred's brother, co-director, works manager and 'right hand man'. The family papers in Alison's care were an invaluable source of information.

Next, thanks go to John Steeds who volunteered to research information in the National Archive records. Information supplied by Alan Brown of the Farnborough Air Services Trust and his contact Geoffrey Cooper is much valued.

Other people, whose assistance is much appreciated are, Derek and Margaret Jerram plus Margaret and Bill Wood for their constructive comments on reading early draft versions; David Healey for his work on the financial facts; David Dykes for initial advice and guidance; Sheila Randall for information on the links between the Haslam family and Morley Church.

In addition, thanks go to the staff of the Derbyshire Record office, the Derby Local Studies Library and the Derby Museums for their assistance. Also, thanks to Picture the Past Derbyshire, The London School of Hygiene and Tropical Medicine, The National Portrait Gallery, WW Winter Ltd plus Christchurch City Libraries, New Zealand for use of their archives and photographs.

This book is dedicated in memory of co-author

**Joan D'Arcy [*1940-2020*]**

Lives and experiences of
Sir Alfred and family in the book
are the outcome of
Joan's comprehensive research.

# Foreword

This is the story of Sir Alfred Haslam whose initiative and business acumen brought about a significant increase in the well–being of citizens, not only in Britain but also other countries. He could be regarded as one of Derby's illustrious citizens for reasons described in the book.

Alfred Seale Haslam was a Derby born engineer who in 1876, at the age of 32, became the managing director of the newly formed Haslam Foundry and Engineering Company Ltd in City Road, Derby.

Alfred made his name and fortune by successfully developing and installing refrigeration systems for ships and cold stores at home and abroad, enabling shipments of frozen meat and other perishable foodstuffs. During the next 50 years the firm prospered with the factory extending and the workforce growing. Alfred, during this time, was proficiently assisted by a brother and fellow director - William Gilbert Haslam.

Creating a regular trade in frozen meat was of national importance and extremely news-worthy. Over the years numerous articles were published in contemporary newspapers, at home and abroad. Online archives have provided an invaluable source of material for compiling the book.

Alfred was also very busy in public life. Locally he was a Councillor and a JP while nationally he became an MP for Newcastle-under-Lyme. In 1891, while Mayor of Derby, he was knighted during a visit by Queen Victoria.

Alfred died in 1927 and the firm was sold to help pay death duties. It became Haslam and Newton Ltd, an amalgamation with a Derby firm. Subsequently, it came under the control of L Sterne Ltd, a Scottish firm, with all activities being removed to Scotland in 1937.

This book covers the trading life of the Company. It describes the factory, the workforce, refrigeration machinery and finally the person who was Alfred together with his family.

# Contents

Acknowledgements iii

Foreword iv

Aerial View of Factory & Money Values x

Introduction 1

Setting the Scene 2

**Part A Trade and Manufacture**

1 **Refrigeration and the British Meat Trade** 6

  Refrigeration 6

  The Meat Trade in Britain 7

2 **Sea Transport** 8

  The Orient Company 9

3 **The Haslam Company 1868 to 1892**

  **Launch & Growth** 12

  The Business 'Takes Off' 16

  A Tremendous Success 19

  Freezing Works and Cold Storage 21

  Accomplishments 22

  Pontifex and Wood 1892 23

4 **The Haslam Company 1892 to 1927**

  **Competition & Stability** 24

  Competition 24

  The Great War 1914 to 1918 26

  The 1920s 27

  Small and Domestic Machines 27

5 **Financial Facts** 30

6 **The Steel Rails Controversy 1880 to 1881** 32

7 **The Union Foundry 1824 to 1868** 34

  Fox Brothers 35

8 **The Haslam Factory 1868 to 1937** 36

  The Factory Expands 38

  Workforce Numbers 43

  Factory Descriptions 43

9 **The Workforce** 48

  Housing 48

  Memories 48

  Workman's Banquet 50

  The Institute and Welfare 51

  **Continued: -**

**Part A continued**

| | | |
|---|---|---|
| **10** | **Refrigeration Machinery** | **52** |
| | The 'Cold' or 'Dry' Air System | **52** |
| | Improved Cold Air Machines | **54** |
| | Vapour Compression System | **55** |
| | The Condenser | **56** |
| | Machines - Ammonia & Carbon Dioxide | **56** |
| | De La Vergne Machine | **57** |
| | Ammonia Absorption System | **57** |
| **11** | **Special Installations** | **65** |
| | Ice Rink | **65** |
| | Air Supply to Blast Furnaces | **65** |
| | Medical Research | **67** |
| **12** | **Potential Sale of the Company** | **69** |
| **13** | **Death of Sir Alfred 1927** | |
| | **The End of an Era** | **71** |
| **14** | **The Final Years 1927 to 1939** | **73** |
| | 1927 Onwards | **73** |
| | Haslam and Newton Ltd | **74** |
| | L Sterne and Co | **77** |
| | Thomas W Ward (Ltd) Sheffield | **78** |
| | E W Bliss Ltd | **78** |
| | Observations on the 'Final Years' | **78** |
| **15** | **Farnborough Cold Air Machine 1935 to 1977** | **79** |
| **16** | **Derby Ice Factory 1899 to 1970** | **81** |

## Part B Sir Alfred and Family

| | Family Photographs | 84 |
| | Preface | 85 |
| 1 | Formative Years | 86 |
| 2 | Alfred's Early Career | 89 |
| 3 | Marriage, Company Growth and Prosperity | 92 |
| 4 | William Gilbert Haslam | 95 |
| 5 | Housing, Property and The Institute | 96 |
| 6 | Service to People of Derby: Mayor | 99 |
| 7 | Children's Fancy Dress Ball | 101 |
| 8 | Knighthood: Arise Sir Alfred | 104 |
| 9 | St Paul's Church, Chester Green | 107 |
| 10 | The Move to Breadsall Priory 1897 | 108 |
| 11 | Alfred's Sons, Coming of Age | 111 |
| 12 | Queen Victoria's Statues | 114 |
| 13 | Newcastle-under-Lyme and Parliament | 116 |
| 14 | Visit to India 1902: Kedleston | 119 |
| 15 | Adventures in Germany: Hilda's Engagement | 121 |
| 16 | The War Years 1914-18: Hilda's Marriage | 124 |
| 17 | Philanthropy and Good Deeds | 129 |
| 18 | The Art Collector | 131 |
| 19 | London Connections | 137 |
| 20 | Literary Connections | 141 |
| 21 | Business and Competition | 144 |
| 22 | Troubled Years | 145 |
| 23 | Eric and Edith - Breadsall Priory | 147 |
| 24 | In Memory | 149 |

**Overall Observations**     **151**

## Appendices Part A

| | | |
|---|---|---:|
| A | Early Day Experiments | 153 |
| B | Arrival of 'The Orient' | 154 |
| C | Arrival of 'The Garonne' | 155 |
| D | Haslam Letters | 157 |
| E | Letter from Mr Ward of J & E Hall Ltd | 159 |
| F | Minutes of Meetings Re - Sale of the Company in 1927 | 160 |
| G | Examples of Financial Accounts | 165 |

# References

| | |
|---|---:|
| Part A | 167 |
| Part B | 168 |

## Information Sources

| | |
|---|---:|
| Information Sources | 169 |

# Figures Part A

| | |
|---|---|
| 1 | Map of Chester Green c. 1927 |
| 2 | The SS Orient |
| 3 | The SS Catania Unloading Frozen Meat 1881 |
| 4 | Haslam Advert January 1882 |
| 5 | Haslam Advert April 1882 |
| 6 | Freezing Works |
| 7 | Complete Small Plant Arrangement |
| 8 | Domestic Refrigerator Advert 1927 - Derby Pure Ice Company |
| 9 | Domestic Refrigerator Advert 1935 - Derby Pure Ice Company |
| 10 | Summaries of Financial Accounts |
| 11 | The Factory c. 1886 |
| 12 | The Factory c. 1910 |
| 13 | Factory Frontage c. 1930s |
| 14 | Factor Frontage c. 1950s |
| 15 | The Pattern Shop |
| 16 | The Erecting Shop |
| 17 | The Iron Foundry |
| 18 | The Smithy |
| 19 | The Coppersmith's Shop |
| 20 | The Pipe Shop |
| 21 | 'SS India' Cold Air Machine at Derby Works |
| 22 | Cold Air Machine Installation New Zealand - Islington Freezing Works |
| 23 | Cold Air Machine for Provision Chambers - Diagonal Type |
| 24 | Cold Air Machine for Provision Chambers |
| 25 | Condenser Assembly |
| 26 | Horizontal Belt Driven Ammonia Compressor with Sizes |
| 27/28 | Steam Powered Ammonia Compressors at the Derby Works |
| 29 | Ammonia Compressor –Electric Drive |
| 30 | Belt Driven Ammonia Duplex Compressor with Sizes |
| 31 | Large Ammonia Duplex Compressor with 3300-volt Electric Motor |
| 32 | Large Four Cylinder Ammonia Compressor Diesel Driven |
| 33 | Duplex Carbon Dioxide Machine - Marine |
| 34 | Motor Driven Carbon dioxide Refrigeration Machine - Marine Type |
| 35 | Refrigerating Machinery for Drying Air Supply to Blast Furnace |
| 36 | Medical Research - Proposed Experimental Refrigerating Plant |
| 37 | Life Cycle of the Haslam Company |
| 38 | Haslam and Newton Prospectus |
| 39 | Refrigeration Compressor – Artificial Silk Works Wigton, Cumbria |
| 40 | Steeping Presses - Artificial Silk Works Wigton, Cumbria |
| 41 | Haslam & Newton Advertisement |
| 42 | Farnborough Dry Air Machine at Derby Works |
| 43 | Derby Ice Factory Advert 1930 |

**1950 Aerial View of the Haslam Factory facing Chester Green.
Looking South West towards Derby
Ex *Crown Copyright***

**Historical Money Values**\*. Money values in the book are for dates between the years 1880 and 1927. To provide a basis for comparing the values, the table below has been prepared using the **National Archives Currency Converter.** Results should be taken as general guide rather than a statement of fact.

| £1 in YEAR | 1880 | 1890 | 1900 | 1910 | 1915 | 1920 | 1930 |
|---|---|---|---|---|---|---|---|
| Equivalent in 2020(£) | 66 | 82 | 78 | 78 | 59 | 29 | 29 |

*\*There is no single measure for comparing historical money values with current values, various methods having been devised to suit particular situations.*

# Introduction

If you travel along City Road in Derby, England, you will see a well-designed brick-built frontage of a factory opposite Chester Green.

On making enquiries you will be told that the factory was once the home of 'The Haslam Foundry and Engineering Company Ltd' owned in Victorian times by Derby born engineer Sir Alfred Seale Haslam.

Sir Alfred [1844-1927] was one of the pioneers in the development of refrigeration systems. He proved to have the technical expertise, the commercial ability and the personality to become a millionaire by successfully manufacturing and installing machinery in ships and cold stores at home and abroad, thus enabling perishable goods - mutton, beef and fruit etc. to be frozen or chilled for shipping across the seas.

The Company was formed in 1876 and trade increased rapidly. Over the years, to cater for this demand, the factory premises and workforce increased in line with production needs. In parallel with commercial activities profits generated by the Company enabled Alfred and his growing family to enjoy an increasingly prosperous life style.

The book describes growth of the frozen meat trade plus the trading and manufacturing operations of the Company. It then continues to describe the lives and experiences of the family members, made possible by the profits of the Company.

# Setting the Scene

Alfred Haslam was born in 1844 and educated in Derby. Alfred's father, William, ran a business as a 'brass founder, bell hanger and smith' employing four workmen. Although the business was small it covered many engineering activities

as shown by the 1843 advertisement. This environment would have given Alfred first-hand knowledge of metal working and inclined him towards an engineering career.

**WILLIAM HASLAM,** St. Helen's Street, Derby (near the New Inn,) BELL-HANGER and SMITH, successor to the late Mr. Hartley. Brass Plates, Rods, Tubes, and Castings to order; Chandeliers, Lamps, old brass work of all descriptions, repaired, re-polished, lackered, or bronzed. Smoke Jacks, wrought iron Gates, Palisades, &c. Balustrades for staircases, in wrought iron and brass. Locks and Keys, all fastenings for doors and windows, and alarm bells of various constructions. Bell hanging on the most approved principles, with the recent improvements, and a variety of original inventions.
*1843 - Stephen Glover's History and Directory of Derby*

Firstly, he served an apprenticeship in the railway works at the headquarters of The Midland Railway in Derby. Subsequently he worked, for 'Allsops' in Burton upon Trent and then, in London, for the Newcastle on Tyne based firm Sir W G Armstrong and Co Ltd, where he gained experience of the design and erection of hydraulic machinery.

In 1868, at the age of 24, in partnership with his father, William Haslam, as Managing Director and financed by a loan from his uncle Joseph Smith, a local farmer, they purchased the Union Foundry at City Road in the Little Chester (now Chester Green) area of Derby. The firm traded as 'Alfred Seale Haslam and Co.' - 'making castings of every description for engineers, millwrights, builders, cast-iron pumps, cheese presses, etc.'

During 1873, after the loan had been repaid, the partnership was dissolved; his father retired and Alfred became owner of the Company. Sadly, his father died five years later so was not able to enjoy Alfred's future success. Some years on Alfred was joined by a brother, William Gilbert, as works manager and Director. He proved to be Alfred's proficient 'right-hand man' throughout the Company's existence.

During Victorian times there was a national concern about a shortage of meat in Britain. On the other hand, in Australia, for example, there was a surplus of mutton as sheep were bred mainly for wool production. Rising prices and growing demand for meat in Britain gave a commercial incentive to develop a method of transporting this surplus across the seas without it being spoiled on long voyages through tropical temperatures. The solution was to design and manufacture refrigeration systems to provide cold storage facilities for transport of frozen meat on-board ships.

With this objective in mind, during 1876, the Haslam business was converted into a Limited Liability Company with Alfred as the Managing Director and principal shareholder. By 1879 a prototype refrigerating machine had been designed, manufactured and transported for display at an exhibition in Sydney, Australia. Then from 1881 ships fitted with Haslam machines were shipping frozen meat from Australia and New Zealand to London.

Orders for machines increased and the business progressively grew. Over several years, the original Union Foundry was replaced by new buildings. More land was purchased, the factory extended and the workforce increased. By the 1890s the site covered several acres. A map [Figure 1] shows the site of the factory adjacent to the River Derwent. The river and canal systems were used, from the early times, for importing raw materials and exporting finished products.

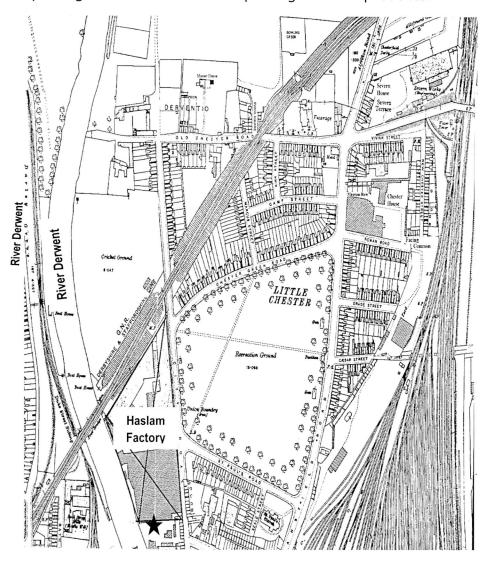

**Figure 1. Map of Chester Green (Little Chester) around 1927 showing site of Haslam Factory. The original Union Foundry was at the southern end of the factory site (Black Star)** *From Ordinance Survey Map*

During 1875 Alfred married Ann (Hannah) Tatam. They started their married life at a house in Duffield Road, Derby. As the Company prospered, they moved to a larger house in Duffield Road and finally to Breadsall Priory a country estate a few miles from Derby. They had three daughters and three sons; all three sons being employed by the Company. Profits generated by the Company enabled Alfred and his growing family to enjoy an increasingly affluent life style.

Alfred was very active in public affairs. Locally he was a Councillor and a Magistrate while nationally he became an MP for Newcastle-under-Lyme. In 1891, while Mayor of Derby, he was knighted during a visit by Queen Victoria*. He died in 1927 and the Company was sold to help pay death duties.

This book is divided into two parts. Part A covers trade and manufacturing activities starting with the motives that triggered Alfred to take an interest in refrigeration.  Part B covers the increasingly prosperous lives and experiences of Alfred and his family made possible by profits generated by the Company.

*Subsequently, Alfred applied for, and was granted, a coat of arms.

# Part A

# Trade and Manufacture

# 1A

# Refrigeration and the British Meat Trade

This section reviews the growth of the ice making/refrigeration industry together with the needs of the meat trade having to keep pace with the growing demand for supplies.

## Refrigeration

When mankind discovered that using ice to chill or freeze food extended the 'shelf life' is lost in the 'mists of time'. Early references to the collection, storing and use of natural ice are mentioned in Chinese poetry[1] dating from 11th to 7th BC. It is also alluded to in the Old Testament[2].

Numerous worldwide references exist in historical records, relating to ice collection, transport and the use of caves or specially constructed ice houses as storage[3]. Britain during the 1700s saw a significant increase in the construction of ice storage houses mainly serving country houses and estates; the ice having been harvested from local lakes and ponds. Examples of these ice houses still exist in Britain.

In the 1800s, to meet demands of an increasing population and the food processing industries, for example, fish, meat, dairy, confectionery and brewing, huge quantities of ice were imported to Britain from frozen lakes in North America and Norway. This was stored in and sold from commercial ice stores in towns and cities. As well as imports to Britain, 'lake ice' was transported, in specially insulated ships, to many parts of the world – including India, Australia and South America.

During this period, engineers were investigating ways of manufacturing artificial ice that would be more economical than natural ice imports.

Scientists, during the previous two centuries, had experimentally demonstrated various scientific principles for producing 'cold' effects and small quantities of ice. Engineers were now adopting these principles to design and manufacture machines for ice-making and refrigeration systems. As time went by greater understanding of the principles came about and numerous patents were registered. As well as Britain developments were progressing with different types of equipment in various countries such as Australia, France, Germany, and America, making it difficult to chart a time line of the progress.

Between 1850 and 1859 eleven British patents for mechanical refrigeration were taken out. From then on, the number of patents increased rapidly. Between 1860 and 1864, ten were granted; 1865-69 twenty; and from 1870-1874 fifty-six[4].

Refrigeration machines needed power to drive them; steam engines being the prime movers plus the associated coal fired boiler plants.

So, by the time Haslam's came into being, during 1868, refrigeration was an evolving business opportunity.

# The Meat Trade in Britain

There was a growing shortage of meat during the 1800s as shown by the following extracts from 'The Meat Trade in Britain 1840-1914' published in 1978[4]:-

> We know that British agriculture was unable to keep pace with the growing demand for meat in the 1870s. The question is, how long before that date was it unable to keep pace with this demand which was fuelled as much by the rise in the level of wages after 1850 as by the increase in population.
>
> Contemporaries were certainly expressing their concern about adequate supplies for the future in the 1860s. This anxiety showed itself in a number of ways. In 1862 and 1863 Doctor Edward Smith presented his reports to the Privy Council on food of the depressed cotton workers of Lancashire and the poorer domestic workers of London and other places. In all cases these reports reveal diets that contained less than 1 pound of meat per week, in some cases very much less than this amount.
>
> The Society of Arts also took an interest in nutrition. In December 1866 the first meeting took place of its Food Committee which was appointed to examine ways of augmenting and improving the nation's supply. At this its chairman, Mr Harry Chester, observed that when he had delivered the centenary address of the council in 1853, he had alluded to the need to devise a means to bring fresh meat into the country from the colonies where a surplus was known to exist. At that time, he had asked why Australia could export only tallow and wool from her sheep and not the mutton itself to feed the masses.
>
> This was a matter in which the society took an active interest from 1863 when it offered a medal and a prize of £70 for the first practical invention that could bring meat from the colonies in a raw state. But in 1866, at the meeting of the Food Committee, Mr Harry Chester asserted that: 'The home supply of meat for the population of these islands is not nearly sufficient for the due sustenance of one half of the population.

Sheep flocks in Australia, New Zealand and the Argentine were primarily bred for their wool rather than for meat. Carcases from surplus stock were either boiled down for tallow or preserved by canning. Apparently other surplus stock could be *"knocked on the head and thrown over cliffs"*.

Consequently, there was great interest in methods by which surplus carcases could be exported to Britain for sale as mutton. Ships fitted with refrigeration systems for storing frozen carcases would enable this to take place.

# 2A

# Sea Transport

An extract from 'The Meat Trade in Britain' reads:-

> ... there was certainly a core of hard-headed commercialism behind some of the attempts to bring fresh meat into the country from overseas sources. The evidence of rising prices and an unsatisfied demand for meat in the United Kingdom gave impetus to much of the activity that went into discovering a feasible method of transporting fresh meat across the ocean from those countries with a surplus.

From the 1870s, several significant events took place:-

An attempt, to ship frozen meat to Britain from Australia, was in July 1873 on the Norfolk. The project was promoted by James Harrison who was one of the Australian pioneers in freezing and ice-making machinery. Apparently, his method was basically an 'ice box'. Pre-frozen meat joints were packed in a tank. This was positioned inside a larger insulated tank. Space between the two tanks contained ice and salt freezing mixture (brine) to produce the refrigeration. There was a pair of tank assemblies. However, during the voyage brine leaked from the tanks and the ice supply ran out causing the meat to be uneatable.

By 1874, a transatlantic service for shipping chilled beef, the relatively short journey, from America to Britain had been established. Beef carcasses were steadily chilled onshore in 'cold' rooms' before being transferred to insulated cargo spaces on board ship. These were kept chilled by a fan circulating air through an ice store. 'Cold' rooms were then used to store the meat at the receiving port.

The success of this method was limited by insulation, ice storage size, distance and climate. This principle was unsuitable for voyages which lasted several weeks and which had to cope with the heat of tropical zones.

An Australian attempt to ship refrigerated meat was made when the Northam sailed from Australia to the UK in 1876. The refrigeration machinery broke down en route and the cargo was lost.

In those days 'frozen' could mean any temperature below freezing point, the end result depending on the design of the equipment and the nature of the product. Now there is a distinction between 'chilled' (just below freezing point 32 degrees F) and 'frozen' (say 20 degrees F and below).

In 1877, French sailing ships, firstly Le Frigorifique and then Paraguay, fitted with steam engine plants to power different types of refrigerating systems, made trial return voyages carrying small quantities of mutton from Argentina to France. Meat from the first voyage (chilled) was acceptable but variable in quality while meat from the second voyage (frozen) was apparently palatable. These trials showed the possibilities of refrigerated ships but, for whatever reasons, no further development or voyages took place, the ships returning to everyday trade[5].

During the 1870s, several firms were developing machines using the 'cold/dry air' process [Chapter 10A]. The firm Bell-Coleman Mechanical Refrigeration Company was the first to develop a marine refrigeration system using this process and took out patents for their equipment in 1877.

After on-shore trials, the system was fitted to the SS Circassia, which made a successful return transatlantic voyage. Later, the SS Strathleven, equipped with Bell Coleman machinery, sailed from Plymouth to Australia and returned from Sydney in November 1879; arriving in Britain during February 1880 with a trial cargo of about 40 tons of beef and mutton in good condition. This trial was the first successful long-distance voyage carrying meat.

Another less publicised event was an Australian financed scheme whereby the chartered steamer SS Protos (Proteus?) was equipped with a duplicate version of a 'Giffard' cold/ dry air machine that had been imported from France. The ship was loaded with sheep and lamb carcasses plus several tons of butter. After a voyage of 65 days from Australia it arrived in Britain early January 1881, the cargo being in good condition[5].

## The Orient Company

During 1878, the year before the 'Strathleven' voyage, the 'Orient Steam Navigation Company Ltd' was created. An abridged Company Prospectus, seeking finance by offering subscription shares was published during 1880 in several papers, for example the *Aberdeen Press & Journal* June 2, 1880.

> ... steamers running between London and Australia and to generally to engage in and develop steam trade with Australia'. Steamers mentioned included The Cuzco, The Garonne and The Orient.

> Further on the prospectus states:- The export of fresh frozen meat is likely to yield an important addition to the company's earnings. A number of applications for space have been made and the necessary refrigerating machines are about to be fitted in the steamers to enable them to carry meat on freight.

Design and manufacture of refrigeration systems and their installation on the three ships mentioned must have been already in progress because; by the end of July 1881, the Cuzco was already in Australia and ready to return to Britain with its cargo of frozen meat. This ship docked in Plymouth in early September 1881.

The Cuzco had been fitted with Bell-Coleman machinery. However, the other two ships mentioned - the Orient [Figure 2] and the Garonne - had been fitted with 'dry air' machines supplied by Haslam and these also returned from Australia, during 1881, with frozen meat cargos, arriving in Britain only a month or so after the Cuzco.

**Figure 2. The SS Orient**

The SS Orient was built in 1879 by John Elder & Co of Glasgow. Commissioned for taking passengers, goods and mail from England to Australia, she was also built to military specifications for use in times of war.

At the time she was the second largest ship in the world at 460 feet long. She was built to run on steam and/or sail.

She was a luxurious ship for first class passengers. Carpets with William Morris designs were laid; there were brass furnishings, elaborate wood carvings and ornamentation of the English Renaissance style, a luxurious music room and saloon.

For the less well-off there was second- and third-class accommodation. She could carry over 500 passengers along with goods and even cattle, as well as the Royal Mail.

She set a London to Adelaide record on her maiden voyage, taking just 37 days and 22 hours. She also set a record for the Plymouth to Cape Town route (17 days and 21 hours), on her second outward voyage.

**Figure 3. The SS Catania**
**landing Australian frozen meat from Sydney in the NW India Docks, London**
***Illustrated London News November 1881***

Another ship, the SS Catania [Figure 3] chartered by the Orient Company, had been fitted with Haslam machinery. The ship docked in England with a cargo of frozen meat in November 1881. The 'Times' newspaper [November 8, 1881] reported the cargo as being 1,033 quarters of beef and 1,469 sheep totalling 110 tons.

# 3A

# The Haslam Company - 1868 to 1892

## Launch & Growth

The foregoing chapters show that, from the mid 1800s onwards, commercial prospects for refrigeration manufacture was an evolving and potentially a profitable business opportunity particularly in relation to shipping frozen goods, successful voyages having been made using 'Haslam' installations by 1881.

It is reasonable to assume that the original Company was created with the aim of taking part in this developing market. It is likely that early in the Company's life, experience and knowledge of refrigeration was being gained alongside 'everyday' production. Likewise, forming a limited company in 1876, presented the opportunity for capital investment from shareholders.

Alfred's chosen method for development of a refrigeration system was the 'cold air' method [Chapter 10A]. The project must have started early in the Company's life because 1882 adverts [Figures 4 & 5] state that the Company had received awards for a prototype machine shown at the Sydney Exhibition held in New South Wales during Autumn 1879 to Spring 1880.

During a speech to his workforce in 1890[14] Alfred reminisced about early times (1880) of the Company. The local press reported:-

> He invited several gentlemen to come down and congratulate him on the success of his invention, but it so happened that during that particular week they had a very sharp frost and a considerable fall of snow. They therefore ridiculed the idea that he was freezing the chamber. They said it was quite cold outside. He thought that was a hard hit, but however they got the temperature inside the chamber many degrees lower than it was in the open air. They then said "Well, how when the water in the tropics is 90 degrees," and he replied they would have no difficulty. They heated water to 120 degrees and still got the same result.

An article in an Australian newspaper [Appendix A] describes two production machines being ready, at the end of 1880, to be shipped early in 1881 to Australia and New Zealand for use in 'freezing works. Prior to this, lengthy negotiations must have been made to gain clients to purchase the machines and contracts agreed.

The chief aim was developing a machine suitable for ships to enable shipping of frozen meat. An article in the Derbyshire Advertiser of August 1881, describes a visit to the works to see a 'cold air' machine in operation:-

> The cold air discharged was noticed to be quite dry and though the machine had been running for about 70 hours the deposit of snow was almost nil......
> We were conducted to a large chamber representing the hold of a ship......
> The temperature of the chamber ranged between 22 to 24 degrees Fahrenheit.

## THE HASLAM FOUNDRY AND ENGINEERING CO., LIMITED,

UNION FOUNDRY, DERBY,

GOVERNMENT CONTRACTORS.     (ESTABLISHED 1824.)

## HASLAM'S
# PATENT DRY-AIR REFRIGERATOR
FOR THE

### PRESERVATION OF MEAT, FISH, FRUIT, VEGETABLES,
ON LAND OR DURING SEA VOYAGE.

Besides Machines for land purposes supplied to Australia and New Zealand, the following Ships have recently been fitted with Machines delivering 40,000 cubic feet of air per hour at 50° below zero:—S.S. "Catania," S.S. "Orient," S.S. "Garonne," S.S. "Catalonia."

ALSO

## MAKERS OF STEAM ENGINES & BOILERS, PUMPING MACHINERY,
### STEAM AND HAND CRANES,
*Hydraulic Presses, Sugar Machinery, Oil Mill Machinery,*
Railway Plant, Contractors' Plant, Cast Iron Tanks, &c.

FIRST SPECIAL MEDAL AND FIRST AWARD AT SYDNEY EXHIBITION, NEW SOUTH WALES.

**Figure 4. January 1882**
*British Trade & Export World*

---

## DRY AIR
# FREEZING MACHINES
### A. SEALE HASLAM'S PATENT.
The most perfect and reliable Dry Air Machine in the market.

The recent arrival of the **S.S. Orient, S.S. Garonne, S.S. Catania,** with 10,000 Sheep, and 100 tons of Beef from Australia, in prime condition, demonstrates the advantage of my system over all others.

**ADVANTAGES.**

No break down by continuous working.
Meat preserved by this Machine secures the highest prices.
Production of a preservative dry air.
No change of temperature in the tropics.
Machines occupy less space than any other apparatus for Refrigerating.

Adopted by the Orient Steam Navigation Company, Limited; Cunard Shipping Co., Limited; The New Zealand Shipping Co., Limited; McIlwraith, McEacharn & Company, Shipowners, London; Messrs. Sloman & Company, Hamburgh Line; Brisbane Meat Preserving Company in Queensland; The New Zealand Refrigerating Company in New Zealand; and other important Shipowners and Meat Preserving Companies in England and Abroad; East and West India Dock Company; R. Campbell & Sons, London and New Zealand; C. M. Mundahl, Esq., Grimsby.

Special Machines made for Cooling Rooms in Wine Growers' Establishments.

SOLE MAKERS—
## THE HASLAM FOUNDRY AND ENGINEERING CO., LIMITED,
# DERBY.
**First Special Medal, First & Second Award, Sydney Exhibition, N.S.W.**

**Figure 5. April 1882**
*British Trade & Export World*

The article finishes with the following:-

> An Engineer of considerable standing, Mr J Campell C.E. of London (who brought the first cargo of meat from Australia per the steamer Strathleven) was engaged on Tuesday and Wednesday, by a number of ship owners in London, in testing the machine and taking the results of experiments. Mr Campbell pronounced the machine to be far in advance of any attempt yet made in mechanical refrigeration and predicates of it that it will be the machine of the future.

As mentioned above, the Orient and the Garonne fitted with Haslam machinery, were returning from Australia with frozen meat cargos during 1881. The Orient, which was considered to be the flagship of the line, arrived at Plymouth on October 3, 1881, only 2 months after the Cuzco; and then the Garonne on October 23, 1881. The ships then voyaged to London to unload.

Five years had elapsed between the formation of the Haslam limited company and the return of ships from Australia carrying frozen meat cargos. During this period, much time and labour must have been used for machinery to be designed, manufactured, tested, and then installed on board; followed by the return voyages to/from Australia. As mentioned previously two machines for land based freezing plants had already been shipped to Australia and New Zealand early in 1881.

Considerable financial investment must have been made by shareholders during this period. It is understood that Alfred and his backers provided sizeable financial surety to the Orient Company on success of the voyages, (£25,000/£30,000 was stated by Alfred during a speech in 1890[14]). This was necessary because there was no insurance cover for the shipping company if the cargoes did not arrive in good condition. [Appendix A]

The Press had been made aware of the impending arrival of the Orient at Plymouth. Several reports were published in the local papers. An example from the '*Western Times*' dated October 4, 1881, is below.

FROZEN MEAT FROM AUSTRALIA

> The "Orient" arrived in Plymouth Sound yesterday afternoon, having about 150 tons of frozen meat consisting of the carcases of 3,000 sheep from Australia. This was the full extent that the accommodation of the "Orient" allowed.
>
> The meat had been preserved by the machine for refrigerating which had been patented by Mr Haslam of Derby. It is different in character from the Bell-Colman refrigerator installed the "Cuzco", which recently arrived in Plymouth, with a like amount of dead meat. The Bell-Colman process is affected by means of snow. In the Haslam pure dry air alone is used.
>
> The two machines have thus been used in successive voyages with a view of testing the superiority of the respective systems. It is understood that the present experience demonstrates the superiority of the Haslam. The Bell Colman machine showed the tendency to choke (with snow) and the meat to discolour. The meat preserved by the Haslam process was tested during the voyage and when it thawed it assumed its original appearance and proved very tender and thoroughly wholesome.

The patentee and representative people boarded the "Orient" on her arrival and were thoroughly satisfied that the invention will enable cargoes of meat to be brought home by the Australian liners in perfectly fresh and wholesome condition. The price at which purchases are made in Australia is about 3½d a pound and can be sold at 5d to 6d profitably.

The experiment may now be considered as being most successfully demonstrated, and it is believed the effect on the English market will in a short time be very appreciable.

Another press report on the Orient [Appendix B] is of great interest as it contains information on:- technical details, satisfaction of the passengers and crew who ate thawed meat during the voyage, together with positive reports from the ship's Chief Engineer on the condition of the meat plus operation of the machinery.

The Garonne arrived about 3 weeks later. A press report [Appendix C] gives information additional to the Orient report. Included is the statement:-

On the voyage out the 'Garonne' took about 30 tons of fresh salmon and various other fish, and this consignment is reported as discharged in splendid condition.

Credit for the first ship to transport meat from Australia must go to the Strathleven in 1878. This voyage was considered as a trial. More significantly, the successful voyages by the Orient Company ships were the start of commercial 'frozen meat' trade between Australia and Britain.

As mentioned previously, in the early days 'frozen' could mean any temperature below freezing point, the end result depending on the design of the equipment and the nature of the product. Now there is a distinction between 'chilled' (just below freezing point 32 degrees F) and 'frozen' (say 20 degrees F and below).

Referring to this distinction between 'chilled' and 'frozen', Mr A Cooper in his book 'World Below Zero' points out that with the Bell Coleman system, used on the Strathleven (similarly on the Cuzco), the cargo would have been be 'chilled'; whilst on the Orient, developments made to re-circulate the cold air around the storage chambers and back through the machinery 'froze' the cargo. Press reports, recorded temperatures in the ship's cold chambers as 18 to 20 degrees F. Subsequently, the Cuzco was fitted with Haslam machinery.

Thus, a claim that the Orient was the first ship to start the voyage from Britain to carry 'frozen' meat back from Australia in 1881 is reasonable.

As experience was gained it was realised that a controlled programme of firstly chilling and then freezing reduced the rate of chemical changes that impair the flavor, so increasing the 'shelf' life of the meat. Also, frozen carcasses would resist knocks and bumps during handling.

British and Australian press reports show that Haslam and Bell-Coleman were both producing and installing cold-air machines for marine use and for 'freezing works' at the same time. Other firms were also 'in the market' but to a lesser amount. Great rivalry and argument resulted with parties accusing each other of copying ideas.

A major controversy was how to deal with the natural moisture in the air as it passed through the machinery. At the 'cold end' of the installation the moisture in the air would become snow and could 'choke' the system. So, to reduce this effect, moisture content of the air had to be decreased before the 'cold end'. This was achieved by cooling the inlet air to the machinery causing moisture to condense out resulting in so called 'dry' air. 'Dry' in this case is only a relative term; the air would never be dry in the absolute sense. However, 'dry air' refrigerator became a term alongside 'cold air'.

Various 'drying' methods were developed by the manufacturers. Rivalry came to a head c. 1884 when Bell-Coleman took legal action against Haslam for patent infringement. Alfred settled this by buying the patents and then taking over rights to manufacture Bell-Coleman machinery. Over time, there were legal actions by other people that Alfred either won or came to agreeable terms.

## The Business 'Takes Off'

The 'coming together', during 1884, of the two main parties would have allowed development of machines incorporating the 'best' of both systems. For several years, the Haslam Company virtually 'cornered' the market for marine refrigeration installations. This was the 'springboard' for future growth and prosperity of the Company. Over the years the factory was extended and a wide range of other products manufactured.

In a very short time scale various companies became customers. The Haslam advertisements of 1882 [Figures 4 & 5] state a significant number of users. Australian shipping lines were soon taking up frozen meat transport. Following the success of the Orient and Garonne voyages the Orient Line fitted Haslam machinery to all their steamers so creating the first shipping-line to go into the frozen meat trade on a regular basis.

A similar pattern of growth happened in New Zealand, for example, by the end of 1884 at least twelve steamships of the 'New Zealand Shipping Company' had been fitted with Haslam equipment to enable regular service of frozen meat cargoes[5].

A notable event for the 'New Zealand Shipping Company', was the Company's first shipment of frozen meat to Britain. During 1881, in Britain, one of the Company's sailing ships - the Mataura - was fitted with Haslam equipment. It sailed from Britain in December. On the outward journey quantities of frozen fish, poultry and game were carried. These were delivered in New Zealand in excellent order. For the return journey the cargo was beef and mutton which had to be frozen on board[5].

The 'Mataura'

Extracts from the Captains log:-

> The barque was being insulated at the fore end and fitted with Haslam's dry air machinery. Mr Haslam was accidentally shut up in a small refrigerated chamber and would have frozen to death had he not been discovered in time.

Left London on December 15, 1881 - Crossed equator on January 15. April 27 1882 - made fast at Port Chalmers wharf, Lyttleton - 150 carcases per day were sent on board and frozen in 'tween' decks for twenty-four hours then bagged and stowed in lower hold. The meat cargo loaded consisted of 3844 carcases of mutton, 24 quarters of beef and 77 pigs: total weight 322,092 lbs, freight £3,340. The voyage home, starting June 12 1882, lasted 103 days and great worry was experienced as the boiler feed pumps would not act on one tack when the ship heeled over. The voyage was a success, and the meat was delivered in an excellent condition[5].

During its construction the Mataura, although a sailing ship, had been fitted with modern improvements including a steam winch and a condenser. Consequently, a steam supply would have been available for driving the refrigeration system.

After reaching New Zealand in 1882, the freezing machinery was inspected by Mr. J. L. Coster, chairman of the New Zealand Shipping Company, accompanied by other notable gentlemen. *The Lyttelton Times* of March 22 reported:-

When the vessel left London the English game, fish, and other perishable delicacies in her freezing chamber were consigned to the residents of Lyttelton, partly as a means of testing the machine and partly for the purpose of providing a novel and agreeable surprise.

The paper recorded that a luncheon was held at the time of inspection:-

The bill of fare was a very tempting one, comprising Labrador salmon, English grouse and partridge. These viands were put on board in London, and had been subjected to various degrees of frost on the passage, but the freezing had by no means impaired their quality, the flavour and delicacy of both fish and game being as perfect as though it had been served in England before being frozen.

It is almost needless to remark that the lunch was most thoroughly appreciated, the viands, especially the game, recalling to the minds of some of those who were present, and who had left England many years ago, reminiscences of the happy days and scenes in the shooting season in the Old Country.

Certain it is that the process adopted on board the Mataura of preserving meat by freezing in no way mars its quality, as it only requires careful thawing to render it in every way precisely equal to the original.

High praises were passed on the excellent quality of the samples on the Mataura table yesterday, and no doubt the lunch will long be remembered by those who had the good fortune to be present. The snow-box in the air-shaft was found a most excellent temporary store-room for the wines etc.

This voyage was the second shipment of meat from New Zealand; the first being by the sailing ship, the Dunedin, refrigeration machinery being of the Bell-Coleman type powered by a specially installed boiler plant. The ship was loaded by the New Zealand & Australian Land Company and sailed from Port Chalmers, in February 1882, only four months before the Mataura.

Another sales opportunity for Haslam was in June 1882. A British company - 'The River Plate Fresh Meat Company Ltd' was formed offering shares for sale. Alfred Seale Haslam Esq was named as the consulting engineer.

The Prospectus[6] stated:-

> The Company is established for the purpose of working the dry air refrigerator; Haslam's patent, in the Argentine Federation and in the adjoining Republic of Uruguay-the great cattle and sheep feeding countries of the River Plate. The patent has already been registered in these countries and the exclusive privilege of working it has been secured by this company. The Haslam Refrigerators have already been adopted and are being used by English and Colonial companies. (six being named)

The Prospectus continued saying there were 70,000,000 sheep in the two countries and gave estimated prices that indicated the carcases could be profitably exported. It continued:-

> Suitable depots will be established as found necessary...... An experienced man will be despatched to South America to erect the depots in accordance with the designs and general instructions of Mr Haslam...... Mr Haslam to supply the machines.

The Company started exporting in 1884. Five years later, in 1889, the following publicity leaflet was issued:-

---

**"Great Success" - Haslam's Patent Refrigerating Apparatus**

At the seventh Annual General Meeting of the Shareholders in the River Plate Fresh Meat Co. at Winchester House, Old Broad Street London the other day, in moving the adoption of the Report the chairman stated that the Board were very glad to meet the shareholders and be able to propose for the first time a dividend. They had been very fortunate in bringing their sheep to this Country and distributing them in perfectly good condition.

Since they had commenced, they had imported more than 1,228,000 sheep and no more than 500 had been condemned.

The whole of the machinery employed by the River Plate Fresh Meat Company up to present date (by which machinery was used to accomplish the above results) for freezing the carcases of mutton in the River Plate and for keeping the carcases frozen on board ship white in transit to this Country was manufactured by the **Haslam Foundry and Engineering Co Ltd of Derby.**

---

The number of frozen carcases imported on ships fitted with Haslam equipment increased rapidly, starting in 1881 from Australia, then New Zealand in 1882 and the River Plate in 1884. In 1881 carcases totalled 17,275 while 9 years later in 1890 the annual total had increased to 2,895,294[14]. On the outward voyages the ships carried cargos of a variety of manufactured goods e.g. linens, calicos, cutlery, tools, etc. along with frozen goods for example, fish, game etc.

# A Tremendous Success

Establishing a successful frozen meat trade was of national importance and as a major newsworthy event caught the interest of the national press, articles being published over several years.

An article in the *Derbyshire Advertiser and Journal*, July 14, 1882, originally printed in the Liverpool Daily Courier, describes a refrigerating system at 'Woodside Lairage' in the docks at Merseyside, Liverpool, ('lairage' being a place where livestock are rested temporarily during transit to an abattoir).

Live cattle were transported across the Atlantic from Canada and the States and then slaughtered in Britain. Slaughtering of cattle had to be regulated according to market demands, and if slack the cattle had to be kept in the lairage and 'fed and watered' for days. Installation of a refrigerating and cold storage system meant cattle could be slaughtered on arrival and the carcases stored in cold stores prior to being sold; it was first of its kind for storage of chilled meat in Britain.

Haslam supplied the machinery and the Dock Board erected four chilling rooms, plus the engine and boiler houses:-

> Mr Haslam who supervised the arrangements explained yesterday to members of the Dock Board, ship-owners, engineers etc the principles of the freezing process and the plan by which the carcases will be preserved for the market. Carcases would be hung for the requisite interval in the cooling rooms and then conveyed by overhead rail to the chilling rooms. These will be maintained at a temperature of 32-degrees F with storage of the meat for up to 28 days without undergoing change.

Each chilling room could store 500 sides of beef. Technical details of the machinery are included in the article.

The *Glasgow Herald* of December 23, 1884, reported that Haslam machinery had been fitted to the SS Elderslie, the first of a fleet owned by a Glasgow firm. The ship had been designed solely for shipping frozen meat. The frozen meat chambers covered all, rather than part, of the vessel. It arrived back in London from Australia during December 1884 with the - *largest importation of frozen mutton ever received in this country; totalling 25,000 carcases and no other freight.* The cargo had arrived in first rate condition and was inspected by a group of VIPs which included Alfred Haslam.

The *Star* Newspaper, February 2, 1884, also published the success story. Cargos other than meat were also shipped using that Haslam equipment. In February 1884 the steamer Ionic left Gravesend. Part of the cargo was a consignment of salmon eggs to be used at 'hatcheries' in New Zealand. The fish were then used to stock rivers. The ship was fitted with a Haslam system. Part of the system had been adapted to provide a climate to protect the eggs. This was achieved by passing saturated air at a temperature of 30 to 34 degrees F at regular short intervals through the egg storage chamber. This was the forerunner of other successful voyages.

In May 1886, the *Pallmall Gazette* gave an account of the arrival of the first shipment of tropical fruit on the steamer SS Nonpareil. The article is a 'colourful' description of a reporter's visit to the ship. Then, in 1888 a cargo of apples from Melbourne arrived in Britain. For these voyages the refrigerating equipment had been modified by Haslam to provide a 'cooling', controlled temperature air flow around the fruit to preserve them. These shipments were the forerunners for regular imports of various fruits and vegetables.

The following year, an Australian newspaper, the *South Australian Register* [January 22, 1887] described how Mr Pullen of North Adelaide had installed a cold air machine at his premises and created three insulated refrigerating chambers under his shop, the first of its kind in the City. The chambers could store 3 to 4 carcases of cattle and 30 to 40 sheep.

> On Friday afternoon, Mr J Hill (Haslam agent) and a number of practical gentlemen visited and saw the refrigerator at work. It performed its duty to the satisfaction of the visitors. The visitors were entertained with iced champagne and frozen fruit from the refrigerating chambers. Mr J Hill took the chair and complimented Mr Pullen on his enterprise. After some conversation upon the advantage of preserving perishable products in our climate the visitors wished Mr Pullen every success and left.

In 1891, at the time of a visit to Derby by Queen Victoria the *Derby Mercury* looked back to 1883, when Alfred entertained Edward Prince of Wales:-

> It is not the first time Mr Haslam has had the honour of entertaining Royalty. He had the honour of being present with the late Chairman of the New Zealand Shipping Company (Mr Coster) to receive his Royal Highness the Prince of Wales on board the Ionic in the royal Albert Dock when the Prince made a close inspection of the vessel, paying special attention to the engine and the refrigerating departments. In the latter he was much interested and Mr Haslam had the honour of showing the Royal Highness the machinery when in mot*ion.*

The *Derby Daily Telegraph* had another 'royal' story to write about in April 1899:-

> It is not generally known that the new yacht being built at Pembroke Dockyard for her Majesty the Queen will be fitted with two special refrigerating machines which have been manufactured by the Haslam Foundry and Engineering Company Ltd. The machines were tested on Monday afternoon in the presence of one of the Admiralty inspectors, with most satisfactory results. (Technical details followed.)

> ... The Company at their works in Derby have also in course of construction a large number of similar machines for battleships, armed cruisers, gunboats and various warships for the British Navy. When these present orders have been completed the Company will have supplied the British Admiralty with about 70 refrigerators of similar types to those above described.

> These refrigerators have been found to be of immense service on board the various ships on which they have been fitted. Giving a continuous supply of fresh meat to the crew and a free supply of ice when required, this, for hospital services on board ship and in tropical climates is invaluable.

Haslam's refrigerators were not confined to cold food storage or to merchant shipping. They came to play a vital role in keeping the crews of the Royal Navy safe. On July 4, 1908, the *Derby Daily Telegraph* published the following article in 'Town and Country Gossip':-

> Eighty of our warships have been or being fitted with Haslam machines and none that will be built in the future will be without them…… there is great

consideration that by means of these refrigerators the ammunition served out to the warships is enabled to retain its power and effectiveness. When cordite is taken into the tropics its efficiency is greatly reduced and is liable to explosion. But by keeping it in a cool chamber where the refrigerating machinery preserves it at a rigid and uniform temperature the risk is reduced to a minimum, and it is found that when it comes to gunnery practice its value is unimpaired from when it left the factory thus securing greater accuracy of shooting.

## Freezing Works and Cold Storage

To cater for the growth of the frozen meat trade there was a need to increase the number of the existing facilities available for freezing and storing meat carcases. In the early days, slaughter would be on the dockside; the carcases then being frozen on board ship. As trade increased combined abattoirs/freezing works were established. [Figure 6]

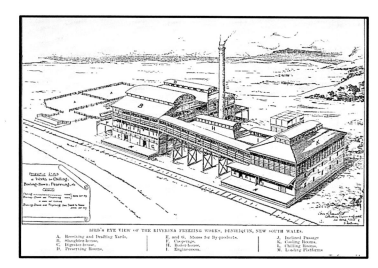

**Figure 6. Freezing Works**

These developments provided sales opportunities for Haslam with orders for land-based plants in Australia and New Zealand. In Australia, during 1881, the first machine was installed at Queensport and in New Zealand at Otaga Bay in 1882 [Appendix A]. Orders for other sites soon followed. As described previously Haslam machinery was used by 'The River Plate Company' in Argentina.

In Britain refrigerated warehouses were constructed to store imported meat, with Haslam and other firms supplying the machinery. During 1881 refrigerated storage was introduced to the Port of London with the opening of a cold store for frozen meat at the Victoria Docks. Then, in 1882, at The West India Docks, a ship hulk, the 'Sea Witch', was fitted with four cold-storage chambers and a dry-air freezing machine supplied by the Haslam Foundry & Engineering Company. The business proved so profitable that a second hulk, the 'Robert Morrison', was similarly fitted[15].

From 1884 onwards, Haslam machines were installed in warehouses; for example - underneath Smithfield Market, at the West India Docks and Cannon Street Station. Glasgow Corporation built new wharves and lairages; the cold stores were fitted with a new design of Haslam cold air machine.

21

# Accomplishments

The *Derby Mercury*, May 6, 1891, records:-

> A few years ago, the Company purchased the Bell-Coleman system of refrigeration and are now sole makers of both versions of the dry-air freezing machines. Their machines have received a large number of gold medals- at the Fisheries, London in 1883; at the International Exhibition Liverpool, 1886; special medal and award at the Sydney Exhibition in 1879; Gold Medal and first-class certificate Calcutta 1884; and gold medal at the Havre exhibition in 1887.

Also, Wyman's Commercial Encyclopaedia, 1888, recorded that 400 of Haslam's refrigerators are in use on land and sea.

By 1891 cold air machines were being used for a wide range of applications. The following is an extract from an article in *'The British Trade Journal'*:-

> The frozen meat trade has been steadily developing - not, however, for meat alone, but for the conveyance of ice, fish, milk, fruit, and vegetables; and we now receive supplies of fresh perishable provisions regularly from Australia, New Zealand, the River Plate, Canada, the United States, and other parts, all of which, with the exception of hardly a fraction, has been brought to us by Sir Alfred's dry-air refrigerating machinery.
>
> Auxiliary to the frozen meat companies for conveying meat, there have been established at all the ports of export and import vast stores of cold-air chambers and cellars, in which the meat and other articles are kept before being placed on board ship or sent to the market for sale to the butcher. The dead meat market at Smithfield is also thus supplied, and such stores are fitted with the Haslam Company's machinery, which works day and night for months at a time, reducing the temperature to the necessary degree.
>
> The Haslam machines are also used for cooling hospitals and public buildings in hot countries, for cooling rooms in breweries, dairies, chocolate factories, and other establishments where a cold, dry air is required. All kinds of perishable food, meat, butter, eggs, milk, and fruit, may be preserved indefinitely whether on land or at sea, in temperate climates or in tropical.
>
> In the bacon curing industry also, refrigerating machinery is of the highest importance, and special machines are made by the Haslam Company for the establishments of wine growers and for the manufacture of ice.
>
> For the last-named purpose the British Government employed them during the Egyptian campaign, and the Italians have used them for a similar purpose with reference to the troops at Massowa.
>
> Among the numerous shipping companies and ship-owning firms who have vessels fitted with refrigerating machinery by the Haslam Engineering Company, are the Peninsular and Oriental; the Cunard; the White Star Line; Messrs. Henderson and Co.; the Orient; the Pacific Steam Navigation; the Shaw, Savill, and Albion Company; Messrs. Donald Currie and Co.; the New Zealand Shipping Company; the British India Steam Navigation Company; the Guion Line, and other important lines.
>
> Of the meat stores fitted with such refrigerators we may mention those at Smithfield, capable of holding about 2,000 tons of meat, and others at the Victoria, the East and West India, and the London and St. Katherine's Docks,

at the establishments of Messrs. Nelson Bros., and at all the leading meat-storage companies' premises. In New Zealand, Australia, and the River Plate, numbers of the machines are at work, as many as twenty being used by a single company.

## Pontifex and Wood 1892

In 1892, the firm of Pontifex and Wood was incorporated. Alfred during the early years had collaborated with the firm. The following extract from a report in the *Derby Daily Telegraph* of October 13, 1892, describes the acquisition:-

> Sir Alfred Seale Haslam has quite recently acquired from the trustees of Messrs. Pontifex and Wood, Farringdon Works., Shoe-lane, London, the plant stock in trade, patterns, drawing, and goodwill of their business which was established a little over 100 years ago.
>
> The concern is perhaps one of the oldest firms of engineers and coppersmiths in the metropolis. They do an important business in the British Isles, as well as a considerable export trade, and their reputation for the manufacture of the Reece patent ice-making machines and refrigerating apparatus on the ammonia absorption system stands exceedingly high. They are also engaged in the manufacture of brewing and distilling plant, sugar machinery and many specialties of importance. The coppersmith's' business is one of the largest in the kingdom.
>
> The transfer of this important industry to Derby is, of course, not a thing that can be achieved in a brief space of time, but every one interested in the commercial welfare of the town will be glad to hear that no undue delay will be allowed to intervene before the gradual removal of the business is proceeded with. Under any circumstances the acquisition of the new concern will give a natural impetus to the general business of the Haslam Foundry and Engineering Co.
>
> The engineering industry of Derby has long made its mark in the markets of the world, and it is to be sincerely hoped that its future may be even brighter than the past. Whilst bridges from our foundries are to be found on every continent, machinery, which Sir Alfred Haslam is associated with and which has revolutionised our food supply, is also produced in our midst. When we say that the firm of Pontifex and Wood gives employment to between 300 and 400 skilled workmen, enough will have been said to show the material importance of Sir Alfred's most recent enterprise to our industrial population,

As mentioned in the extract, the firm manufactured refrigerating systems using the ammonia absorption process [Chapter 10A]. They were also leading experts in distilling plant both domestic and large industrial types capable of processing large quantities of liquid.

# 4A

# The Haslam Company - 1892 to 1927

## Competition and Stability

## Competition

The great number of cold/dry air machines in operation proved their effectiveness. However, an article in an Australian publication [*Queensland Country Life*, January 1904] apropos freezing works, states:-

> From 1893 onwards as the meat trade increased it became abundantly evident that cold air machines must give way to something less costly in the labour upkeep and coal consumed per ton of frozen meat prepared.

A more economical method of refrigeration was the vapour compression system using ammonia as the refrigerant [Chapter 10A]. From the early 1880s, manufacturers worldwide had developed the system, initially for ice making and then by the late 1880s machines were well established and used for land-based installations for example, freezing works and cold stores.

Initially, ammonia was not considered acceptable for marine installations because of the need to have a reserve store of ammonia together with the possibility of ship movements, in heavy seas, leading to harmful leakage of ammonia from broken pipes and joints; hence the preference for the cold air machine. Over the years, manufacturers introduced improvements and during the 1890s ammonia machines had been installed on ships and shipments of frozen meat completed.

Another system developed during the 1880s was the carbon dioxide compression system; this gas was non-flammable and therefore suitable for marine installations. These operated using the same principles as the ammonia type but at much higher operating pressures. Both the ammonia and carbon dioxide machines were physically smaller and more efficient i.e. for a given duty used less steam than cold air machines.

Therefore, during the 1890s, the cold air process existed alongside ammonia and carbon dioxide systems. 'Ammonia types' mainly for use on land based freezing works and cold-stores with 'carbon dioxide types' mainly for use in marine refrigeration. To compete with other firms Haslam's' developed and manufactured these types of machines, resulting in the gradual decline in applications for cold air machines.

During the early decades of the 1900s, the Admiralty remained a long-term user of Haslam cold air machines. On their ships, they preferred the machines as they were robust, of straightforward construction, and being self-sufficient with no need to store either carbon dioxide or potentially hazardous ammonia in case of emergency. Steam for driving the machinery would be from the ship's main boiler system, the amount used was small relative to the steam used to power the ship.

The following two advertisements indicate that Haslam started to advertise ammonia machines between 1890 and 1895; ammonia machines [De La Vergne system, Chapter 10A] being mentioned only in the 1895 advertisement.

**HASLAM'S** DRY-AIR FREEZING MACHINES,

*Made under the Haslam & Bell-Coleman Patents.*

USED FOR THE PRESERVATION OF FOOD ON BOARD SHIP AND ON SHORE.
ADOPTED BY THE LEADING SHIP OWNERS AND MEAT COMPANIES IN ALL PARTS OF THE WORLD.

HASLAM'S Cane Mills and Sugar Machinery.
HASLAM'S Hydraulic Presses for all Purposes.

SPECIAL MEDAL and AWARD, Sydney Exhibition, N.S.W. | GOLD MEDAL, Fisheries Exhibition, London, 1883
GOLD MEDAL, Liverpool Exhibition, 1886.      |       „        Calcutta      „      Calcutta, 1884.
                  GOLD MEDAL, Havre Exhibition, 1887.

The HASLAM FOUNDRY & ENGINEERING Co. Lim. Derby.

Telegraphic Address: 'ZERO, DERBY.'                [4]

**1890**

Telegraphic Address "ZERO, DERBY." ESTABLISHED 1821. Telephone No. 50. A. B. C. Code used.

The Haslam Foundry & Engineering Company,

INCORPORATED WITH                           LIMITED,

PONTIFEX & WOOD, LONDON,
UNION FOUNDRY, DERBY,

AND 34, NEW BRIDGE STREET, LONDON, E.C.

Makers of HASLAM'S DRY AIR FREEZING MACHINES, used for the Preservation of Food on
board ship and on shore; adopted by the leading Shipowners and Meat Companies in all parts of the world.
Makers of ICE-MAKING MACHINES AND REFRIGERATING MACHINES on the Pontifex
and De-La-Vergne system.
SUGAR MACHINERY, DISTILLING PLANT, BREWING PLANT, STEAM AND FIRE
COPPERS, HYDRAULIC AND SCREW PRESSES of all kinds, IRON AND BRASS
FOUNDERS, COPPERSMITHS, &c., &c.                                9

**1895**

During 1899 a newspaper report (*Derby Daily Telegraph* April 25) on a works visit mentions that several ammonia compression machines were under construction. One machine was described as:-

> … claimed to be one of the largest refrigerating machines ever built. It is destined for a large new freezing works in the River Plate where the Haslam's company have installed a number of machines during the past 15 years. [Figures 26 & 27]

By 1901, carbon dioxide compression systems were also in manufacture. An advert in *The Morning Post* on August 30 describes the firm manufacturing the three types of systems viz-cold air, ammonia and carbon dioxide machines.

# The Great War 1914 to 1918

World War 1 - 'The Great War' - began in August 1914. In December 1914, a press review of the effects of the war on Derby firms[8] shows that prior to the war the Company had a full order book:-

> The Haslam Company has been running full time, dealing with numerous orders for refrigerating machinery. They commenced the year with big contracts from New South Wales and their production is to be found on a number of our merchant steamers. The war has affected their usual trade but an optimistic view is taken of the future.

By 1915, the military demand for artillery shells was far greater than could be supplied. To help meet this urgent demand the Government asked firms to undertake production. In late 1915 the Haslam factory was adapted to assist the war effort. A building was erected so that part of the factory could be turned over for production of shell cases.

With so many men at the front there was the need for female workers to take their place. Harold Cox's mother left Darley Mills to work in the shell shop, turning brass shell cases, a precision job which involved careful use of gauges.

Another young woman, Gladys Finley, had to change her job in millinery for war work. She was given the task of inspection. When a shell case passed her scrutiny, she would use a metal die to stamp a serial number on the base of the shell case.

Alfred's nephew, Gerald Haigh Haslam (son of W G Haslam a brother of Alfred) was brought back from the army to manage the shell shop. Previously he had been an engineer in the factory designing and installing machinery. He courted Gladys Finley and they were married in 1917[7].

The Company were also involved with manufacture of guns. In a letter to a fellow businessman [February 1918] Sir Alfred mentioned a large volume of war work which has recently largely increased. Then on March 12 1918, he wrote:-

> The Government are sending a large quantity of machinery here to assist to double the output of guns, and to make matters worse they have pressed me to against my wishes to open up a factory in the town to turn out a large quantity of bombs which we are starting next week [11].

With the date being only few months before the Armistice in November 1918 most likely the bomb factory never came into being.

This 'Relic of the War' cutting is from the Derby Daily Telegraph October 23, 1935. By that date L Sterne Co. Ltd would have been controlling activities in the works. Mention is made that the machine was used in connection with the manufacture of guns in the Great War.

## RELIC OF THE WAR
### OLD PLANING MACHINE REMOVED FROM DERBY WORKS

A 100-ton planing machine was yesterday removed from the works of the Haslam Foundry and Engineering Co., Ltd., City-road, Derby, for transportation by the L.M.S. Railway to Sheffield.

The machine has been at the foundry for 30 years, and during the Great War was used in connection with the manufacture of guns. It has a base 30 feet long. It is now considered obsolete.

The company has disposed of it, and it was to-day removed in sections to St. Mary's goods wharf, Derby.

Only one similar machine of anything like the same size now remains in the town, and it is at the works of Messrs. G. Fletcher and Co., Ltd.

# The 1920s

After the Great War, trading continued steadily with general improvements being made to the refrigeration machines. A 1923 Haslam catalogue stated that:-

> We have made important improvements in the design and construction, and have thoroughly tested and put on the market, high speed silent running ammonia compressors and carbon dioxide machines. About 3100 machines are in use at the present time in various parts of the world for the following purposes -

There followed a list totalling 23. As well as ice making, other uses included were for:- the **cooling of** beer, chocolate, gelatine, oil, lard, water for chemical works; the **storage of -** hops, dairy produce, eggs, fish, furs, fruit and hotel provisions; the **drying** of air for blast furnaces, photographic plates and grain in flour mills; **freezing -** meat, fish, rabbits etc.

By this date the machinery could be powered by electric motors or diesel engines, either belt driven or mounted integrally with the refrigerating machine.

## Small and Domestic Machines

During the 1920s, development work was progressing with the design and manufacture of equipment for retail and domestic application. A factory visit was made by the Institution of Mechanical Engineers. Quoting from their report:-

> The great popularity of small refrigerating plants has been met with a simple and efficient machine of which large numbers have been installed.

Most likely the plants referred to would have been the type on show at The Royal Agricultural Show at Leicester in 1924 and described in the July 4 issue of 'The Engineer'. It was described as a small self-contained mechanical refrigerator working on the ammonia compression system. The complete plant comprised the ammonia compressor, a condenser, the cooling pipe arrangements being inside the insulated chamber. At the show the power was from a diesel engine, the alternative being an electric motor.

The plants were suitable for use in large houses, hotels, restaurants and tradesmen's shops. An example is shown in Figure 7. A claim made was that to operate a chamber of 175cu ft capacity (say 5x 5ft square and 7ft high) it would cost only about 5 shillings a week.

Another section of the visit report quotes:-

> The works are now organised for the mass production of domestic refrigerating plants, the demand for which has greatly increased owing to the restrictions imposed on the artificial preservation of food.

This refers to Public Health Regulations prohibiting use of preservatives in dairy, meat and drink products, formally introduced in 1927, resulting in the need to store food in a suitable environment.

At that time domestic refrigerators would have been of the 'ice box' types. These comprised an insulated cabinet with a block of ice held in a tray or compartment near the top of the cabinet. Cold air circulated down and around storage compartments in the lower section. Provision was made to collect the melted ice water at the bottom of the cabinet. The ice had to be replenished by delivery from an 'ice supplier'. In Derby, this type of refrigerator was sold, along with regular ice supplies, by the Derby Ice Factory. A 1927 advertisement is shown in Figure 8. These types of refrigerator were still in production in 1935 but as Figure 9 shows competition from electrical units had started.

**Figure 7. Complete Plant-suitable for shops & hotels etc.**
**Small enclosed type machine; direct expansion air cooler and cold chamber**
***Haslam Leaflet c. 1925***

THE

# DERBY PURE ICE
AND
# COLD STORAGE
CO., LTD.

Will Supply and Deliver

## Ice Free of Charge

FOR ONE MONTH

**TO EVERY PURCHASER**
OF A
## Houshold Refrigerator

**whether supplied through us or any other dealer,**

AND WILL THEREAFTER KEEP THE REFRIGERATOR REGULARLY REPLENISHED WITH ICE

**at a charge of from**
**per week 3/- per week.**

**Be Prepared for keeping Your Food under Proper Conditions in the Coming**
**SUMMER.**

**The New Public Health Regulations prohibit the use of preservatives, consequently it is in the highest degree advisable that every householder instal a**
**REFRIGERATOR.**

**There is Nothing Better or Cheaper than ICE.**

The VALUE IN FOOD SAVED will more than compensate you for the small outlay.

CALL AT THE COMPANY'S OFFICE, IN THE MORLEDGE,

AND INSPECT OUR SPECIAL SAMPLE ICE BOXES, FROM £4. HIGHEST QUALITY. LOWEST PRICE.

**Figure 8. Refrigerator Advert**
***1927***

*The above illustration shows a few types of—*

# ICE REFRIGERATORS

The prices of these vary from £4/15/- to £6/10/- each only, and we can recommend them with the utmost confidence.

**ICE IS NATURE'S REFRIGERANT,** it gives just that degree of humidity which is so essential, and these boxes will give you as good results as the much advertised Electric Models, and at an infinitely less cost.

**HOUSEHOLD REFRIGERATION** is now in vogue, but before you decide on the type of Refrigerator you require call and inspect our models.

## ICE CREAM

We have also a wonderful little **ICE CREAM MAKER** with which you can make your own ice cream in 30 seconds. An ideal accessory to the Ice Refrigerator. You should really see this unique little appliance. Only 36/-.

# DERBY PURE ICE & COLD STORAGE Co. Ltd.

MORLEDGE, DERBY. Phone 201

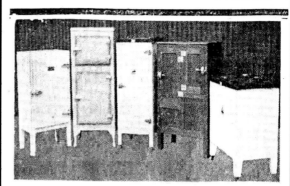

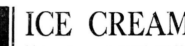

**Figure 9. Refrigerator Advert**
***1935***

# 5A

# Financial Facts

A ledger[11] exists which contains the annual accounts for the Company from its formation in 1876 up to 1901.

Accounts for the beginning and the end of the 1876-1901 period are compared in Appendix G. They show how the Company had flourished through this period with a healthy bank deposit, significant investments and a reserve fund. The existence of a Workman's Insurance Fund, which first appeared in the 1898-99 accounts, indicated that the firm took an interest in workforce welfare.

In some years, as well as share dividends, bonuses were also declared these ranged from £2,200 to £6,800. Who received these is not clear; it most likely was the workforce?

The charts [Figure 10] prepared from the ledger show how the Company fared during this period.

- The sales showed a steadily rising trend along with the trading profit.

- The 'spike' in sales for 1880-81 was basically due to a ledger entry named 'Materials Rails' - purchased for £118,588 and subsequently sold for £121,734 the profit being around 75% of the trading profit for the year. These figures were unusual being considerably higher than the other sales and warranting an individual entry in the annual profit and loss accounts. (See the next chapter - The Steel Rails Controversy.)

- Dividends paid to shareholders varied in line with the profits and averaged £9,000 annually.

- The net revenue which is a measure of the worth of the Company progressively increased, the value in 1901 being around £70,700.

A minute book[11] for the later years of 1915 to 1927 records dividends varying between £12,500 to £17,500 with an average of £16,000 indicating that the Company was still in good shape up to the final year of 1927.

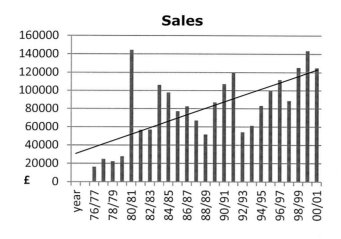

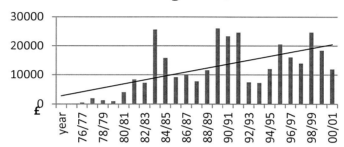

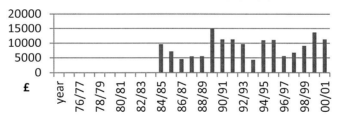

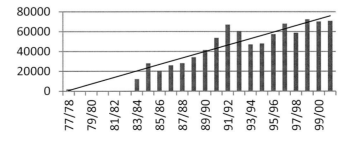

**Figure 10. Summaries from Company Accounts 1876-1901**

31

# 6A

# The Steel Rails Controversy 1800 to 1881

Referring to the previous comments [Chapter 5A] on the sales 'spike' shown in the 1880-81 accounts, connected with the purchase and sale of '*materials* rails' Research revealed that the customer was the Queensland Government in Australia.

At that time Queensland was one of the six self-governing British Colonies in Australia. Events, leading up to the purchase and delivery of the rails generated controversy and intrigue resulting in an official inquiry by a Select Committee in Queensland and subsequently a private Royal Commission in London. A series of interlinking events occurred; the main ones being outlined below.

- In September-October 1879, an order for the supply of rails and fittings was agreed, in Queensland, between the Government and a representative of an English company (Ibbotson & Co Ltd), the order being subject to ratification by the firm.

- In October 1879, the Queensland Premier (Mr. Thomas Mc. Illwraith) left, on business, to travel to England via America, primarily to finalise a loan sanctioned by the Queensland Government, secondly enquiring into the working of the Agent General's office* in London and, to finalise the rail purchases.

- On his arrival in England in December, the Premier found the provisional rail contract had not been ratified due to increased prices of rails and fittings.

- In January 1880, the Premier, on his own responsibility, instructed the Agent General to ask for tenders for the supply of 15,000 tons of rails. Seven firms were invited to submit tenders, with the Haslam Company subsequently obtaining the contract at £9 18s 6d per ton.

- The Premier had found during dealings with the London office that the Agent General and his Secretary (Mr. Hamilton) were not working as a team with very little verbal communication between them, using clerks to pass messages. The office administration and the filing was disorganized with the staff being unclear of their duties.

- This resulted in Mr. Hamilton being dismissed from his position. He took exception to his dismissal and complained in letters to the Colonial Secretary in London who passed them on to the Queensland Government. (NB. The Agent General resigned later during 1881.)

- In his letters, Hamilton protested that he had been suddenly dismissed by the Premier without notice or compensation, and even without a reason. He insisted that the contract for the rails had been let without his knowledge.

- He claimed matters regarding the tenders had been settled by the Premier, the Agent General and Mr Ashwell the consulting engineer for the

Queensland Government. Hamilton pointed out that Ashwell had been a shareholder in the Haslam Company at its formation. Also, Ashwell was brother in law of the Premier thus implying that Ashwell could have influenced the tender decision.

- He made the point that two of the largest firms that manufactured rails had not been invited to tender. He had information that these firms could supply rails for a much lower price (£6 per ton was mentioned) than that quoted by the Haslam Company, who were not rail manufacturers. (*However, they would have been capable of making various fittings needed for assembling the rail track.*) This implied that accepting the Haslam tender had cost the Government extra expense - a sum of £60,000 being quoted.

- Another matter was that tenders were invited for the transport of the rails to the colony on the condition that it would by 'full ships direct' (i.e. only rails and not any other cargo). This was unusual as lower prices would have been quoted for ships carrying other cargo in addition to rails.

- The successful contractor for the transport was 'Mc. Illwraith, Mc. Eachern and Co', a company owned by the Premier's brother Andrew, one in which the Premier was also a shareholder. As well, there was a potential conflict of interest because the Premier and Mr. Ashwell were registered as owners of shares in vessels fulfilling the contract - so implying favouritism.

- These allegations of misconduct by the Premier and members of his Ministry were presented in a petition to the Queensland Parliament in July 1880. This led to a bitter controversy and exploited by the Opposition.

- A Select Committee was appointed to investigate with the majority dismissing the allegations. The Opposition objected to these findings resulting in a private Royal Commission being established, during 1881, in London. Alfred Haslam was one of the people called to give evidence. The outcome was that there had been no collusion or favouritism and charges brought against the Premier were without foundation.

*Sources of information:-*

Petition to Queensland Parliament - *Telegraph* (Brisbane) July 10, 1880

Report of Select Committee - *Darling Downs Gazette* November 11, 1880

Report of Royal Commission - *Capricornian* July 9, 1881

*Agent General - the representative in England of the Queensland Colony

# 7A

# The Union Foundry

## 1824 to 1868

The Union Foundry purchased by William and Alfred Haslam in 1868 was situated in City Road, Derby. The road was lined with small industries; a silk mill, colour works and iron foundries all making use of the river. The Union foundry was the most northerly of these enterprises and lay just within the town boundary on the east bank of the River Derwent, a short distance upstream from the town centre. Beyond, were open fields, most of which was farm land. This was an area known as Little Chester, now Chester Green. Little Chester was a separate township, until its incorporation into the town in 1877 with most of the land belonging to the Corporation of Derby.

The foundry was one of the earliest started in Derby. It had been established in 1824 by Joseph Faulkner (or Falconer), who had been employed previously by Messrs. Strutt of Belper. At first trading as Falconer & Co. he later went into partnership with William Peach. [Pigot & Co commercial directories 1828-9, 1835, *p*79]

The foundry was ideally situated, with ready access to the essential raw materials for the manufacture of iron products. Iron smelting blast furnaces had been established in 1780 and 1818 at Morley Park, only five miles distance while coal from mines to the north, at Kilburn and Ripley, was off loaded directly at the riverside factories or at nearby coal wharfs.

By 1843, Falconer & Co. was a well-established and versatile company as appears from Stephen Glover's *History and Directory of the Borough of Derby*:-

> This company is in high repute for their domestic and engine castings. At this factory are manufactured all sorts of kitchen ranges, stove grates, patent mangles, furnaces, pans for bleachers, dyers and brewers' pots and kettles, plain ornamental palisading and tomb railings, bookcases and garden rollers, also castings for millwork and machinery, water-wheels and engines, pumps, gas and water pipes, and spouting for factories and housing. [Glover pp80-81]

Edward Falconer followed his father into the business but after his death in 1845 his executors advertised the foundry for sale with quite a detailed description. It occupied an area of 1,200 sq., with an adjoining small yard. Its situation by the Derwent, which was navigable for flat bottomed barges, gave it access to the Trent via the adjacent Derby canal and there was 'a very superior wharf'. The foundry itself comprised two casting houses and associated workshops, a warehouse and a counting house, three cranes, two cupolas with blowing apparatus, a drying stove and a 7-horse power condensing engine. There was also attached, a row of ten cottages, known as Union Street, or Court No. 3 in census returns, one of which was the Tiger pub and another the watchman's house. [*Derby Mercury* November 26, 1845]

34

Afterwards, William Peach carried on the business with his son, as William Peach & Son. The 1851 census recording that 42 men were employed, and trade continued to grow as the firm acquired a reputation for the excellence of its castings. However, in 1858 they decided to sell the foundry and it was purchased by the Fox Brothers.

# Fox Brothers

**Fox Brothers Foundry**

Fox Brothers was a firm of tool and lathe makers, occupying a stretch of the river bank a few hundred yards downstream from the Union Foundry. They would have been much gratified by Glover's description of their business:-

The stranger, who has a taste for examining excellent workmanship and ingenuity, would be much gratified by going through Messrs. Joseph and James Fox's manufactory, City-road; these gentlemen manufacture the best lathes ever produced in any country, which are sent to all parts of the continent. [Stephen Glover, 1843]

The firm used the Union Foundry to carry on the production of castings for their special kind of work. Unfortunately, in c. 1866-7 the business came to an end in Derby, the machinery and patterns being scattered all over the country, though Fox Brothers carried on in business in Nottingham for years with considerable success. The failure of the business could have been due to either financial problems or a flood which inundated properties on the River Derwent in 1866.

# 8A

# The Haslam Factory

## 1868 to 1937

A few letters to Alfred from his father William have survived, written between 1867 and 1868, which refer to Alfred's progress from one firm to another. [Appendix D] In a letter dated April 6, 1867, Alfred's father expresses surprise that Alfred wished to leave his job at Armstrong's in London. Further correspondence must have taken place on this matter because a year later in a letter dated May 12, 1868, Alfred's father writes:-

> I send you advertisements of the sale of premises and Foundry late "Fox brothers". The Foundry is a good opening for anyone who thoroughly understands the business, but I do not think tool making at Derby has been a very good trade of late some years ago it was a first class affair, but other towns of late taken the lead I think Foxes were behind the times, and the great flatness of trade has given the finishing stroke, and perhaps there has been a want of economy.

> If you were ready to begin the foundry seems a good choice that is if you had a knowledge of the details of the business, but I fear it would be too great and too speculative an undertaking under present circumstances.

**Union Foundry Sale Notice**
*Derbyshire Advertiser & Journal May 17, 1867*

Notwithstanding this doubt a quick decision was made to agree to the purchase as his father had acquired the Union Foundry by July 4, 1868 [*Derby Daily Telegraph* January 6, 1927]

The firm traded as the 'Alfred Seale Haslam & Company'. In Harrod's Directory 1870 it was advertised as making - castings of every description for engineers, millwrights, builders etc., cast-iron pumps, cheese presses, horse racks and mangers etc.

On January 11, 1873, the partnership between Alfred and his father was formally dissolved by mutual consent. Alfred then took the position as Managing Director. [*London Gazette* January 11, 1873]

Only one month later, on February 17, an unfortunate incident occurred when, late in the evening a fire broke out in one of the foundry workspaces. Alfred's quick thinking and resourcefulness probably saved the foundry from being entirely destroyed. The story was graphically recounted in the *Derby Mercury*:-

A fire broke out at Mr. Haslam's Union, Foundry, City Road, Derby on Monday night, and though it was a late hour when the flames were discovered, a large crowd of persons, attracted to the glare caused by the fire, assembled on the spot. Mr Haslam went round the premises shortly before ten o'clock, and saw nothing amiss and the watchman also went on his round at ten, but all was safe at that time. The engine fires had previously been extinguished, and there was no light on the premises.

The watchman had not been away many minutes; indeed, he had barely sat down in his house and commenced his supper when an alarm was raised. This would be about half-past ten o'clock. The residents of the neighbourhood were at once in a state of great consternation, especially those who occupied the houses in Union Street, which is adjacent to the foundry. Information was speedily sent to the Town-hall, and the hose was conveyed to the scene of conflagration.

The flames appeared to spread with wonderful rapidity. From St Mary's Bridge the scene was imposing; the foundry adjoins the river, and the effect of the reflection of the burning pile in the water was very striking.

It was found that the fire had broken out in a three-storey building and in the bottom storey. This was used as a grinding shed, the second storey being the pattern shop and the upper portion of the building being store rooms for patterns. The foundry yard was filled by a crowd of spectators, whose object appeared to be to create confusion by their varied shouts and cries.

The hose was quickly attached to hydrant in the street and Mr. Haslam took it in hand, and mounted one of the sheds overlooking the engine-shed, which adjoins the burning building, and which had by this time caught fire. He directed the water onto the rafters and afterwards into the body of the shed.

In the engine-shed, a number of barrels of oil and tallow were already being consumed and, as the joists on the principal part of the foundry penetrated the walls of this building, it was feared that the fire would extend beyond limits if not arrested.

Mr Haslam displayed much presence of mind and great courage and continued to pour the volumes of water on to the engine-room until there was a visible effect, and the flames were considerably subdued. Meanwhile Mr. Haywood and the firemen arrived with the Niagara engine, which was backed towards the river, into which the pipes were laid.

After a few minutes the pumping began and the jet was played upon the remainder of the burning pile. By this time nearly the whole of the patterns and the pattern tools were consumed. The gable, having lost the support of the main joist which after trembling fell into the flames, began to bend in the middle and finally gave way with a tremendous crash, carrying with it the greater portion of the side wall.

After more than an hour the fire was under control. The estimated damage is £1,000, and we understand that the building which has been consumed, was insured in the Guardian Fire Office for £800. It was fortunate that the flames did not reach the foundry itself. Had they done so there would have been no chance of saving the premises or the adjoining row of houses, the loss would then have been £7,000 to £8,000. Work at the foundry cannot be resumed for two or three days, and orders of several tons of castings will be delayed. [*Derby Mercury* February 19, 1873]

The foundry was only saved from total destruction by the lack of wind and 'the rapid arrival of hose from the Town Hall'. The newspaper poetically recorded the 'impressive sight of flames reflected in water'. The loss was insured but many patterns were destroyed. It was a tough beginning.

## The Factory Expands

During 1876 the business became a limited liability company:- the 'Haslam Foundry and Engineering Co Ltd'. The above-mentioned *Derby Daily Telegraph* article [January 6, 1927] gave the registration date as December 13. The first shareholders under the articles of association were London Engineers and comprised apart from Alfred as Chairman, representatives of the old well-established firm of Pontifex and Wood, and the then rising firm of Appleby Brothers, whose intention was to contract much of their heavy class work as possible to Derby. Mr J J Robins, who was for many years with Mr James Haywood at the Phoenix Foundry, was the first secretary of the Company.

Records[16] held in the National Archives at Kew show the Company had a nominal capital of £100,000, in £100 shares, the initial subscribers' being:-

| | |
|---|---|
| Alfred Seale Haslam, Derby, engineer and iron-founder | 80 shares |
| CJ Appleby, Emerson Street, Southwark, engineer | 10 |
| Joseph Jessop, Leicester, engineer | 10 |
| Edmund A Pontifex, Shoe Lane, engineer | 15 |
| John Barton, Shoe lane, engineer | 15 |
| William Henry Ashwell, 26, Cauldwell Street, Bedford, engineer | 10 |
| Harry William Nield, 3, College Road, Brighton, engineer | 1 |

The number of directors was not to exceed seven, nor be less than three. Qualification was 10 shares. The first six people in the above list were named as directors. A General Meeting would decide remuneration. Mr. A S Haslam was appointed managing director for ten years, at a salary of £500 per annum for the first five years, afterwards-at such increased salary as may be mutually agreed between him and the directors.

In the 1878 edition of Wilkins and Ellis Directory the Company is described as - *The Haslam Foundry and Engineering Co. Lim. Iron Founders Engineers and Boiler Makers.* It was still producing steam engines and boilers, hydraulic presses, pumps, cranes and smaller items such as machine tools.

There was no mention of refrigeration but design, development and manufacture must have been in progress and sales agreed because, as described previously by the end of 1880 the first two production machines were ready to be shipped.

In the early 1870s the Great Northern Railway Company put forward a plan to construct a railway line to connect the East Midlands coal fields and industries, via a station in Friar Gate Derby, to the industries of Burton upon Trent and beyond. The idea appealed to the Corporation and by 1875 a belt of land was sold and the line was under construction, running diagonally across fields to the north of the Union foundry on a high embankment. This left a 'wedge of land' between the two. [Figure1]

One of the objectives of the recently created Haslam Company must have been to increase and modernize the workshops and offices because in 1877 finance was available for purchase of the 'wedge of land' from the Corporation for £1,000 an acre. Designs for a new factory, extending northwards, were prepared by architect Julian Young.

The workshop initially would face the rough ground of the Chester Green Common. The Derby Corporation had for some years had desired to convert this to a modern recreation ground or 'Green'. Money raised from the sale of land to the Great Northern Railway Company made this possible. This could not be done without an Act of Parliament and it was not until Saturday, November 4, 1882, that a ceremonial beginning was made. A grand procession of 24 carriages assembled outside the Town Hall to convey the dignitaries through cheering crowds to Little Chester, with Alfred amongst them as Ward Councillor. On arrival, the Mayor of Derby, Abraham Woodiwiss, cut the first turves and provided an ox roast.

The project took four years to complete. The land was uneven and prone to flooding and the Haslam Company freely supplied tons of waste foundry material to raise and level the ground.

The Green is seen in the foreground of the drawing [Figure 11]. Around the perimeter were iron bollards, linked by chains, manufactured by the W. Abell foundry on Brook Street, Derby. The ground was further encircled by London planes and lime trees while seats were placed for spectators to watch cricket and other sports.

The opening ceremony took place on May 15, 1886. It was to have been held on the Green but it had rained so hard that it was moved into the Guildhall. In a speech during the ceremony Alfred said that in later years they would be thanked- *for the "lungs" they had provided in the midst of what must ultimately become a populous district.'* Many industrialists, Jesse Boot, for example, spent much money on providing sports grounds for their employees. For the Haslam workforce it was provided on their doorstep by the town council.

From 1882, as the new Green was being constructed, the new foundry was extended northwards to designs of architect Julian Young. A drawing [Figure 11] shows the frontage to the Green, an impressive red brick facade with large, multi-paned, cast iron and arch-headed windows. The River Derwent which could be navigated to this point by flat bottomed barges and, as shown in the drawing, was used to transport coal and other heavy goods to and from the foundry. Across the river was the GNR trans-shipment wharf, offering another ready means of transport, though the line was not directly accessible from the works[7].

The Company expanded rapidly and by 1891 the foundry had been extended further to 44 bays so that it now abutted the GNR line, a six-foot-wide strip of land being reserved as a pedestrian access to the railway bridge across the Derwent. The architect, Richard Waite of Duffield, simply continued the existing facade, adding a further 18 windows: the extension join is visible but the bricks are a close match[7]. During 1892, the London firm of Pontifex and Wood was incorporated with Haslam's. To cater for the new business workshops were built behind the main foundry and in 1894 new offices were built. A print of the factory is in Figure 12 and views of the factory frontage are shown in Figures 13 & 14.

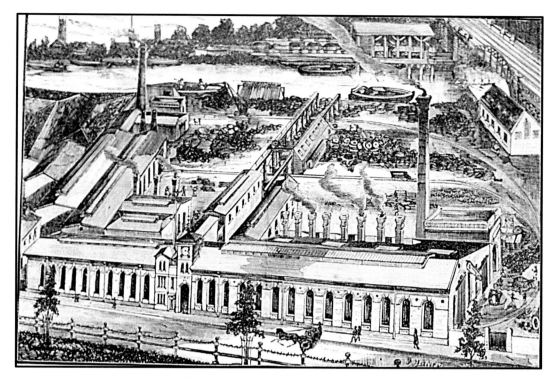

**Figure 11. The Factory c. 1886**
*The Royal Album of Arts and Industries*

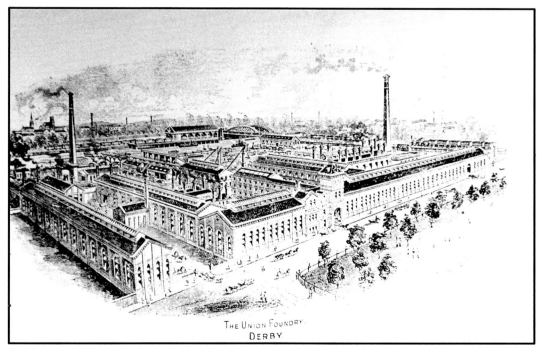

**Figure 12. The Factory c. 1910**
*1923 Haslam Catalogue*

**Figure 13. Factory Frontage c. 1930s**
*Picture the Past Derbyshire*

**Figure 14. Factory Frontage c. 1950s.**
**Owned then by EW Bliss (England) Ltd**
*Picture the Past Derbyshire*

## Workforce Numbers

A *Derby Daily Telegraph* article, July 4, 1908 reads:-

> Mr Haslam started in business 40 years ago with 16 men and boys. He has in his possession a wages book from which we learn that wages paid at the end of the first week totalled £13.13s.2d.

Going forward, the 1881 census entry for the family states Alfred was an - *Iron-founder and Engineer employing 150 men and 40 boys*. During his speech, in 1890, at a Workman's Banquet Sir Alfred stated a figure of 462 employees, not including crews at London, Glasgow, Liverpool and other places.

Census returns for the Chester Green area confirm the company's expansion. The acquisition of the business of Pontifex and Wood in 1892 would have resulted in more staff- *between 600 and 700 are being employed* being mentioned in the report of the Institution of Mechanical Engineers Meeting held in Derby during 1898.

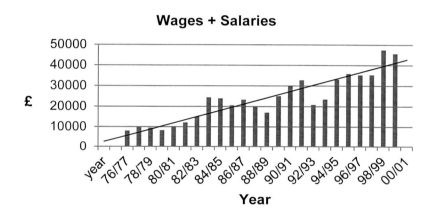

This chart has been prepared from the annual accounts covering the years 1876 to 1901[11]. It demonstrates the steadily upward trend in wage costs over the years as the workforce increased from 16 in 1868; to 190 in 1881; around 500 in 1891; then between 600 and 700 in 1898.

However, moving forward to 1937 when under the control of L Sterne & Co Ltd, the announcement was made of the removal of manufacturing to Scotland with the closure of the Derby works. A press article reported that some 170 men would be affected.

## Factory Descriptions

Descriptions of the factory and machinery were published over the years. Examples of these are:-

In 1898, the **Institution of Mechanical Engineers** held their annual meeting in Derby. Several factories were visited including Haslam's'. Quoting:-

> The works occupy an area about 4 acres...... They extend from City Road to the banks of the Derwent and contain extensive fitting shops with average spans of 70 feet...... with foundries for making castings in iron up to 15 tons and brass castings of considerable size...... A large business is done in the manufacture of apparatus for breweries, distilleries, vinegar making, and milk condensing; and coppersmiths' work in all its branches.

Around 1898 a publication *'Derby-Illustrated'* described the works as follows:-

> The works comprise foundry forges, pattern shops, fitting-rooms, machine shops, stores and offices, and the whole place is equipped with powerful and improved machinery for the rapid output of all descriptions of engineering work. Turning machines, lathes, steam hammers, etc., are in constant activity in every direction, and the power is supplied by three powerful steam engines, while over 500 experienced hands are employed in the various departments. Boilers of all descriptions are made, and every kind of hydraulic apparatus, hoists and mill machinery.

> The manufacture and erection of the famous refrigerating appliances occupies a prominent place, and the greater part of this work is done in the front part of the works, the large foundry occupying the rear of the premises.

> The Union Foundry is, in fact, among the most complete in the kingdom, and forms one of the most important elements in the modern industrial character of Derby. Indeed, the name of the town has become famous throughout the world as the centre and seat from which emanate the Haslam refrigerating machines. No better site could have been selected for these important works, as the proximity of the two great railway lines and the river Derwent, with its connected network of canals, affords the greatest facilities for the transit of heavy goods.

> The most complete arrangements are provided at the Union Foundry for the prompt turning out of all classes of machinery and engineering work, and, under the personal supervision of Mr. W. G. Haslam (brother of Sir A. S. Haslam), every machine and part turned out is subjected to the most rigid inspection and testing. The output is enormous, and the business is rapidly extending.

## The Iron and Steel and Allied Trades (Buxton meeting 1910)

> The works, however, are by no means limited to the production of refrigerating plant. They form, rather, a colossal foundry and engineering establishment dealing with work of every description and on the largest scale.

> The foundries and workshops are of approved modern design, more substantially built than a typical factory, but conforming in the main to the accepted principles of modern factory architecture in point of lighting, spaciousness and the orderly placing of the several shops. They are uniformly of a single lofty storey, lit from the both sides and roof, and. amply ventilated'.

## Boring Machine

> During 1913-14 - to suit manufacturing needs, a special cylinder boring machine was designed and built within the factory; the designer being Mr J F Bradshaw, the assistant works manager. The machine-in-design will deal with all types of cylinders within its capacity both efficiently and accurately. It will cater for cylinders 4ft.6in diameter bores by 7ft.6in.long and 6ft.9in over the flanges. [*Derby Daily Telegraph* May 23, 1914]

## Information in the 1923 Haslam Catalogue

The three erecting and machine Shops, which occupy a frontage of around 730 feet are exceptionally commodious with an average span of 70 feet and fitted with all modern cranes and lifting arrangements, enabling weights of up to thirty tons to be dealt with.

The machine Tools are of the highest class, and include the most modern labour-saving devices, all electrically driven. Work of the best kind only is undertaken and the machinery manufactured by the firm has a reputation for accuracy and good finish. A department has been added for the manufacture of all kinds of pipe coils and grids on a large scale. This is equipped with pipe-welding plants on the electric and oxygen-acetylene systems. Also, the most improved pipe coiling and bending devices have been installed.

Workshop photographs from the 1923 catalogue are shown in Figures 15 to 20.

Figure 15. The Pattern Shop

Figure 16. The Erecting Shop

Figure 17. The Iron Foundry

Figure 18. The Smithy

Figure 19. The Coppersmith's Shop

Figure 20. The Pipe Shop

# 9A

# The Workforce

## Housing

Subsequent to the formation of his Limited Company, Alfred needed to increase his workforce to cope with an increasing workload. At that time the Green was being developed and City Road was being extended with land becoming available for housing. To attract skilled men Alfred purchased land, at the North West Corner and during 1880 began to build small terraced houses. During 1885 he built a row of houses on the East side of City Road then more houses were built on Old Chester Road during 1886. Between 1884 and 1891 prestigious houses were built along the newly constructed St Paul's Road. Details and photographs of the housing developments are described in Part B of the book.

By building decent quality houses around Chester Green for his workforce, Sir Alfred, by coincidence, helped to create a close-knit community which lasted well into the twentieth century.

## Memories[7]

The foundry opened up opportunities for steady employment for the young school leavers of Little Chester. *'I have put you in line at the foundry'* were the words used to tell 14-year-old Tom Harrison that his uncle had put his name down for an apprenticeship as a bench moulder. No argument was allowed. He had already found employment at Moore and Eady's but after six months he took up a seven-year apprenticeship at the foundry. There was a Haslam foundry school and Tom was taught his trade there by Mr. Spooner, who did not give him an easy time. At the end of his seven years he received his first wage packet of £2/1s/7d.

Apprentices were not expected to strike for any reason. When there was a strike at St. Mary's goods wharf in 1911 the 'lads' gathered to watch at the gate, only to be drenched with water by the police who turned hoses on them[7].

Work was hard and hours were long, beginning at eight o'clock when the bellman began to toll the work's bell. This was a challenge to some of the local lads, like Harold Cox of 16 Camp Street. They would dare each other to be last inside before the bell ceased ringing and would race across the Green and attempt to dart inside the closing gate. When the bell stopped, the gate was shut and late comers had to enter through the office door and explain themselves, losing 15 minutes of pay.

Many of the jobs, like pattern making and moulding, were skilled and the workers had a special status, symbolized by their clothing. The moulders, for example, wore a white apron with moleskin trousers, black coats and bowler hats and always carried an umbrella to work, or so it is said.

A fitter was another skilled worker. Harold Cox recalled that his father was a pipe fitter or 'bender'. His mother's ancestors were the Woods of Old Chester Road and his grandfather George was a foundry labourer.

The success of the foundry opened up new horizons for local young men. Henry Edward Bates, who grew up in the former toll house on Mansfield Road, found himself unexpectedly at sea, sailing with the 'China' to San Francisco in 1890 as a maintenance engineer. In the summer of the same year he was again at sea, maintaining the refrigeration units in the 'Handel' as it sailed to New Zealand. His career was cut short in 1892 with his tragically early death at the age of 34.

**Discharge Certificate for Henry Bates
by permission of trs Ida Neale nee Bates**

His son Thomas William Bates was one of many boys who became apprentices at the foundry. He worked there as a pattern maker in 1910, later moving to the nearby Handyside foundry. His most notable achievement is that he is the only man known to have walked round Chester Green on his hands. Clearly work at the foundry was an excellent way of developing strong arm muscles.

Local boys followed their fathers into the firm. A typical example was Herbert Rhowbotham who lived in a Haslam built house (97, City Road) and worked as a lathe operator for most of his working life. He obtained an apprenticeship for his son, also Herbert, in 1926.

Another skilled job was blacksmithing. Peter Land's grandfather, who lived at the corner of Marcus Street and Camp Street, was a foreman blacksmith. He remembers how:-

> Many times, as a small child I used to go and meet him and walk home with him. I know that the dreadful working conditions that I saw as a child influenced me greatly in my later life. There was only an earth floor where he worked and the washing facilities comprised a bucket into which he put a piece of red-hot iron to heat the water for himself and his striker.

# Workman's Banquet

Alfred was appointed Mayor of Derby in 1890. As a celebration for this event he arranged for a banquet to be held for employees and their wives. It was held in the specially decorated Drill Hall Derby and about 750 people enjoyed the social gathering[14].

When the mayoral party entered the Hall, around 5.30pm, they were received with loud and continuous cheering as they took their seats.

It was an extravagant eight course meal starting with oysters, followed by soup, fish, entrees, removes, roasts, sweets and desserts. Musical entertainment was provided during the evening by an organist, and glee singers.

At the end of the meal, after the Royal Toasts, Mr Prince, the principal works foreman and a popular long-time member of the staff formally presented an illuminated address to Alfred (*Loud Cheers*) on behalf of the staff. Alfred in reply thanked the employees and in particular the wives. He reminisced about the Company and their achievements. Alfred, then thanked Mr Prince for his twenty-three-and-a-half-year faithful service and presented him with a marble timepiece having the inscription - 'Presented to Mr Henry Prince by the Mayor of Derby (A Seale Haslam, JP) Dec 20th 1890' (*Loud cheers*).

During a toast Alderman Roe praised Mr. W.G Haslam (Alfred's brother) as a good person anyone could find. Alfred could not always be present at his works, and he (Mr. Roe) did not know anyone in whom he could place more confidence. W. G. Haslam said in his reply that he had always strived to promote the interests of the men. *(Hear, Hear.)* He thought one of the main duties was to endeavour to ease distress, and do the utmost to make lives of the men happier and more comfortable by every means possible. *(Hear Hear).* After other speeches and toasts the event ended with singing of the National Anthem.

**Derby Museums Archives**

### Toasts.

| Proposer. | Toast. | Responder. |
|---|---|---|
| THE MAYOR. | The Queen, the Prince & Princess of Wales, and the rest of the Royal Family. | |
| | GOD SAVE THE QUEEN. | |
| | THE MAYOR'S ADDRESS. | |
| GLEE | "Christmas Bells." | |
| SIR W. EVANS, BT. | Bishops, Clergy, and Ministers of all denominations. | Rev. CANON KNIGHT. Rev. JOHN HASLAM. |
| GLEE | "Slumber song." | |
| JOHN BAILEY, ESQ., J.P. | Army, Navy, and Auxiliary Forces | GEN. SIR HENRY WILMOT, BART. COL. BUCHANAN. |
| GLEE | "Comrades in Arms" | |
| SIR JNO. MONCKTON. | The Mayor and Mayoress. | THE MAYOR. |
| QUARTET | "Brightly dawns our Wedding Day." | |
| ALD. H. H. BEMROSE, J.P. | The Town and Trade of Derby. | ALD. W. HOBSON, J.P. |
| GLEE | "Little Jack Horner." | |
| T. ROE, ESQ., M.P. | The Staff and Workmen of The Haslam Engineering Co., Ltd. | W. G. HASLAM, ESQ. |
| GLEE | "Come where my love lies dreaming." | |
| THE MAYOR. | The Visitors. | W. J. PIPER, ESQ. |
| GLEE | "Good night, beloved." | |

The *Derby Daily Telegraph*, December 22, 1890, gave a detailed account of the proceedings and a full description is included in Part B of the book.

## The Institute and Welfare

Alfred took great interest in the welfare of his own employees. During the 1890s, he had an elegant building of 14 bays erected, with brick pilasters, curving round the corner. This was at the corner of St Paul's Road and City Road. The architect was James Wright of 23, St. James' Street.

Upstairs was an industrial space for pattern rooms. On the ground floor an entrance hall led into a reading room, with a large room to the rear to cater for workers' educational and recreational needs[7].

The *Derby Mercury* for December 9, 1896, published a report about a tea and concert held at the Institute:-

> A tea and a concert were held in the recently erected Haslam Institute on City Road. The institute has been built by Sir Alfred Haslam at considerable cost…… For a long time the workers have wanted a place to hold social gatherings…… The building is a very spacious one…… In the daytime it is used as a mess room and in the evenings for literary/recreation…… it is managed by a committee of employees.

> Quite 300 sat down to a substantial tea and there were about twice that number at the subsequent concert…… Amongst those present, besides Sir Alfred and Lady Haslam were the Bishop of Derby plus other members of the Haslam family…

> After tea the Bishop of Derby briefly addressed those present…… He hoped they would make the place as successful as possible…… He hoped that the young men would go there at night  so to be kept away from the curses of drink and gambling, which was the ruin of many (Hear hear)…… Sir Alfred was loudly applauded on rising, he said he had built the place for two purposes; one to be used as a mess room for the workmen and the other for their enjoyment…… and to bring along their wives, sons and daughters (Applause)…… He was glad to see that short religious services were to be held once or twice a week. He had promised to supply a harmonium and he expected it to arrive next week (Applause). The concert programme was of a varied character and all the performers acquitted themselves admirably.

# 10A

# Refrigeration Machinery

### The 'Cold' or 'Dry' Air System.

(a) An extract from a Haslam catalogue:-

The diagram below shows the working of a cold air machine. The suction pipe of the air compressor C draws the warmest air from top of cold chamber; this is compressed, thus increasing its temperature, and delivered into a tubular cooler D, cooled by water circulated around the tubes and delivered into the expansion cylinder E, when in expanding and assisting to drive the compressor the air gives up heat in the form of mechanical work and is thereby reduced to a temperature of about 80 degrees F. below zero. The cold air is delivered into the opposite side of the cold chamber and circulates through ducts in the chamber, thus completing the cycle. To further cool the compressed air, and thus cause it to deposit its moisture, a second cooler or patent Dryer can be fitted in which the return air from the cold chamber to the compressor passes around the tubes, the moisture deposited being drawn off by cocks or valves. A prime mover e.g. a steam engine drives the air compressor. The air expander piston is connected by a crankshaft to the drive system. As the air expands it moves the piston, so providing a supplementary drive for the compressor.

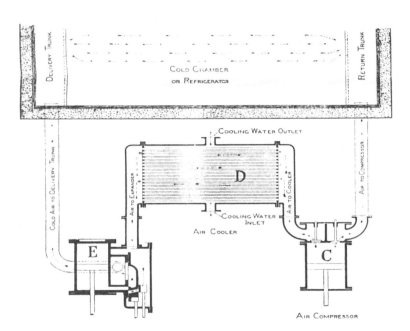

### (b) How Meat is Artificially Frozen - *The Illustrated Sydney News*- February 18, 1882.

> The question of meat exportation to Europe has, as everybody is aware, become successfully solved by the adoption of what is termed dry-air refrigeration, the carcases being artificially frozen and kept at a temperature below Fahrenheit's zero during the whole of the time occupied by the voyage.

> The machine by which this result is brought about is known as Haslam's dry air refrigerator, of which we give an illustration. Its action is based on the well-known circumstance that when air or other gas is compressed, and afterwards expanded, cold is produced. The air enters at the pipe A, and is

immediately conveyed to the cylinders below, marked B. Here it is compressed to 40 lbs per square inch an operation which raises the temperature to about 200 degrees F.

After compression the air is conveyed to the left-hand refrigerator R, where, by the circulation of cold water in copper tubes, the temperature is rapidly reduced. It suffers a still further reduction in the right-hand receptacle R' and is then expanded in the metal box X. (This box, although several inches thick, is covered at one end with a thick coating of hoar frost from the

THE FROZEN MEAT TRADE—DRY AIR REFRIGERATOR

condensation of aqueous particles in the external atmosphere). The air then passes through ducts to circulate around the freezing chamber. W is the steam cylinder which sets the machine in motion. The cold actually produced is sometimes as low as 80 below zero, but usually the temperature in the freezing chamber is about 40 below zero.

The patentee claims the following advantages in using this machine:-

1. It occupies less space than any other apparatus for producing cold on a large scale.

2. The meat, fish, or other food which is preserved by its use is kept in such good condition that it will command the highest prices.

3. The air used is perfectly dry, at no part of the process does it come into actual contact with water; indeed, in the second refrigerator R' any particles of aqueous vapour remaining in it are frozen.

4. There is no difficulty in maintaining any degree of cold in the hottest climate.

There are other advantages which will immediately occur to anyone used to sea transit. The tons of live-stock required for a large vessel occupy with their food so much space that it is not difficult to believe a statement made to the effect that the space so saved pays twice over for working the machine. It is also said more steam was required for distilling water to assuage the thirst of the cattle carried on the ship than is wanted to work the new machine.

# Improved Cold Air Machines

Several types of 'cold air' machines were designed and manufactured and a few examples are described below.

The December 4, 1896, issue of 'The Engineer' reports on a new ship - 'The SS India' - constructed for the Peninsular and Orient Line. Haslam's had installed the refrigeration machinery in the aft end of the engine room. A photograph of the machine taken at the Haslam works is shown in Figure 21. The machine could discharge 80,000 cubic feet of air per hour at a temperature ranging from minus 50 to minus 80 degrees F below zero.

A large hold at the aft end of the vessel was specially fitted for carrying frozen meat, besides this there were compartments for the storage and preservation of cargoes, such as butter, fruit, and other perishable food-stuffs. In addition, there were cold chambers for storage of provisions for use by the crew and passengers en route. The storage rooms were insulated using the best approved system.

The cold air was discharged into the insulated rooms, where any temperature could be maintained, depending on the nature of the cargo, in the individual compartments.

This type of machine was manufactured in sizes capable of producing 20,000 to 200,000 cubic ft of air per hour. Machines of this pattern could be used either on land based or marine installations.

This kind of machine appears to be used for the cold air installation, Figure 22, at the New Zealand Refrigerating Company's Islington Freezing Works. The picture (c. 1890) shows the original Haslam combined steam engine and compressor. It was installed at Islington in June 1889. Later it was converted to an ammonia compressor which was in use well into the twentieth century.

A Haslam brochure (c. 1894) includes other examples of cold air machines. [Figures 23 and 24] These types were to provide refrigeration for provision chambers on board ship. Quoting from the Haslam literature:-

> The principal use of these machines on board ship is for preserving fresh provisions for the passengers, thus doing away with the carrying of livestock. The machines are very compact and designed so that they can be placed "tween" decks.

# Vapour Compression System

## (Ammonia or Carbonic Acid (Carbon Dioxide) Refrigerant)

The principle of refrigeration using the vapour compression system is outlined below:-

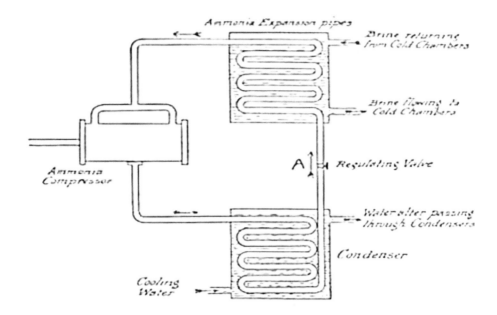

**Compressor** - The refrigerant is drawn into the compressor in the form of a gas, at a pressure which varied according to the temperature required in the refrigerator, and was then compressed to such a pressure as is necessary to liquefy it, depending on the temperature of condensing water.

It is then passed into the **condenser** coils, where the heat developed by compression was dissipated by means of cold water passing over the exterior surface of the condenser pipes. The gas, being cooled under pressure, condenses and collects in the bottom coils as a pressurised liquid.

The liquid then passes through the **Regulating Valve**, which provides a restriction causing a pressure drop. When passed into the **Refrigerator** coils, the low-pressure liquid refrigerant expands back to a gas, and in so doing takes up heat from the surrounding liquid e.g. brine. It was then passed back to the compressor ready to begin the cycle again. (Brine, typically, was a solution of calcium chloride and water, the freezing point of which is below 32 degrees F.)

The carbon dioxide system uses the same principle as above with a much higher pressure being required. Typically pressures in the ammonia system could be around 150 to 200 lb/sq. in. while in the carbon dioxide system pressures could be up to around 1000 lb/sq. in. Compressors would be driven by prime movers: initially steam engines and later by electric motors or diesel engines.

Broadly speaking there are three methods by which the 'cold' produced is transferred to the cold storage chambers. In the above diagram the cold brine is circulated through a pipe circuit in the cold store. The second system is 'cold air circulation'. A fan circulates air across an array of 'cold brine' pipes; known as a 'battery'. The cold air is then passed through ventilating ducts around the cold store. In the third method the cold refrigerant is circulated directly around a circuit of pipes in the cold store. This third method is the principle used nowadays for domestic refrigerators using modern refrigerants.

## The Condenser

A major part of the refrigeration process was the condensing system. Several types of condenser systems are depicted in the 1923 Haslam catalogue. An example is shown in Figure 25. This is an assembly of nine sections, each of twelve individual 'double pipe' condensers, the 'double pipe' being inner and outer concentric tubes. Cooling water passes through the inner tube in the reverse direction to the ammonia gas in the outer tube. This contra flow ensures the ammonia is cooled down as near as possible to the temperature of the cooling water and the ammonia condenses into a liquid for recirculation in the refrigeration process.

The numbers of individual condensers used was dependent on the condensing capacity required for the particular application.

## Machines - Ammonia & Carbon Dioxide

Various ranges of sizes and types of machines are illustrated in the 1923 Haslam Catalogue; some examples are given below.

A double acting horizontal ammonia machine is shown in Figure 26 together with a summary of size and capacity range. The version shown is belt driven; other examples are shown as being powered by steam or electricity.

Figures 27 and 28 shows works views of large machines each comprising two horizontal ammonia machines coupled to a triple expansion vertical steam engine. The machine had a refrigerating capacity of 200 ton and was built for the River Plate Fresh Meat Company. (The refrigerating capacity being a theoretical measure of the amount of ice a machine could make in a 24-hour period.) An electrically powered ammonia machine for a New Zealand installation is in Figure 29.

An example of another range of ammonia machines - 'The Duplex Enclosed Type' - is shown in Figure 30. Views of this type of machine driven by electric motor and a diesel engine are shown in Figures 31 and 32.

Haslam's had started producing carbon dioxide machines by the early 1900s. Over the years the types on offer increased and a variety of machines are shown in the 1923 catalogue. Two examples illustrated in the catalogue are shown in Figures 33 and 34.

## De La Vergne Machine

This machine was manufactured by the De La Vergne Refrigeration Company in New York. By the late nineteenth century, the Company specialized in the manufacture of large vertical ammonia compressor systems, steam-driven, and employing banks of condensers. The first installation in Britain, under licence, was by L Sterne Co Ltd for the Leadenhall Market Co in 1887.

Haslam's must have obtained agreement for manufacture of this type of machine as the system was being advertised including a woodcut in a Company brochure (c. 1894). An article in 'The Engineer' for February 19, 1897, records that this type of machine was manufactured and installed by Haslam's in a new cold store at the North West India Dock in London; the store having a capacity of around 378,000 cubic ft.

Horizontal ammonia machines, developed by Haslam and other manufacturers, proved to be more efficient in power consumption, cost and space than the De La Vergne system causing orders for this type of machine to decline.

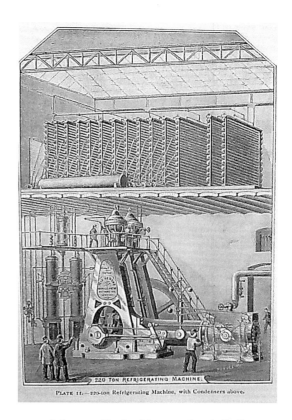

PLATE II.—220-ton Refrigerating Machine, with Condensers above.

**A Large De La Vergne Installation**
*Haslam Literature DRO*

## Ammonia Absorption System

This type of refrigerator makes use of the fact that ammonia dissolves extremely well in cool water but not so well in hot water.

In an absorption cycle refrigerator, a concentrated solution of ammonia in water is heated in a boiler until most of the ammonia is driven out of the water as a high-pressure gas. This hot, dense ammonia gas then enters a condenser, where it gives up heat to its surroundings and becomes a cooler liquid. The liquid ammonia then enters a low-pressure evaporator, where it evaporates becoming a cold gas acting as the refrigerant. This evaporation process draws heat out from the evaporator and refrigerates everything nearby. Finally, the ammonia gas is returned to the boiler to begin the process again.

The return phase makes use of the absorption process, in which the ammonia gas is allowed to dissolve in relatively pure, cool water. The gas dissolves easily in this water and thus maintains the low pressure needed for evaporation to continue in the evaporator. The now concentrated ammonia solution flows to the boiler where the ammonia is driven back out of the water under pressure and everything repeats. Pontifex and Wood Ltd became leaders in this type of equipment. It was particularly suitable for industries where steam heating was already available and being used for processing, for example, breweries and dairies.

**Figure 21. Cold Air Machine for the S.S. India, at the Derby Works**

Constructed on what is the duplex system. It can be worked either as a whole machine or, if repairs are needed, either side can be worked independently. Each side of the machine has a steam cylinder, an air compressor, an expansion cylinder, and a water pump. The engines work at 160 lb/sq in. steam pressure. A steam condenser in the bed plate is fitted in connection with the engine. The machine is also fitted with integral air, water circulating and boiler feed pumps.

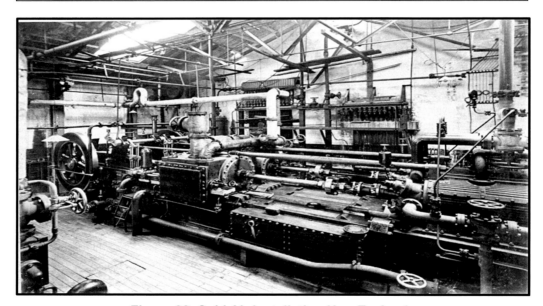

**Figure 22. Cold Air installation New Zealand**

The original Haslam combined steam engine and compressor at the New Zealand Refrigerating Company's Islington Freezing Works. c. 1890. This 'cold air' refrigerator was installed in June 1889. It was later converted to an ammonia compressor which was in use into the twentieth century
*Christchurch City Libraries, File Reference: CCL PhotoCD17 IMG0086*

The diagonal machine is made in sizes to deliver 10,000 to 12,000 cubic ft or air per hour. It is compact, self-contained and very accessible on-board ship. The machine consists of compound high- and low-pressure steam drive cylinders and one air compressor mounted on top of the bed and one air expansion cylinder fixed upon the end, with the water pump, air pump and feed pump bolted on the side of the bed

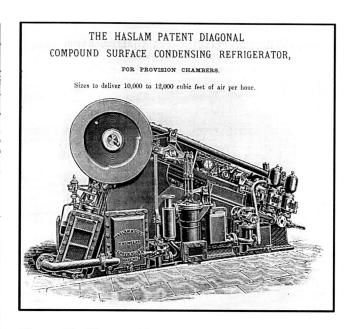

**Figure 23. Diagonal Dry Air Machine for Provision Chambers**
*Haslam Literature DRO*

This type of machine is made in sizes varying from 8,000 to 12,000 cubic ft per hour. It comprises one steam drive cylinder and one air compressor mounted horizontally and one air expansion cylinder fixed vertically upon a box bed, on which the horns are cast for main bearings of the crankshaft. The bed is cored internally for the air cooler, the reservoir and patent drying pipes.

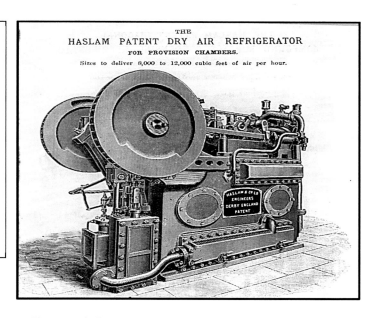

**Figure 24. Dry Air Machine for Provision Chambers**
*Haslam Literature (DRO)*

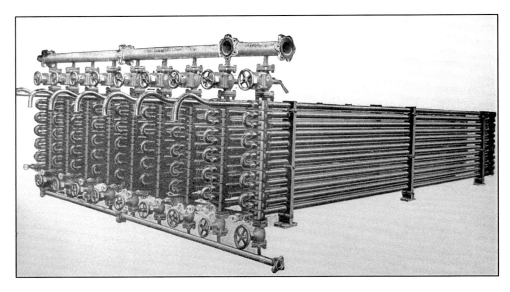

**Figure 25. Example of a Condenser Assembly**
*Haslam 1923 Catalogue*

**Figure 26. Horizontal Belt-Driven Ammonia Compressor**
*Haslam 1923 Catalogue*

| Size Range | 4A | 10 |
|---|---|---|
| Refrigerating capacity- tons per 24 hours | 7.5 | 33 |
| Horsepower | 12 | 51 |
| Flywheel Diameter inches | 72 | 108 |
| Revs per minute | 115 | 80 |
| Overall Width inches | 50 | 78 |
| Overall Length inches | 116 | 189 |
| Weight ton | 2.75 | 7.5 |

**Figures 27. & 28. Rear and front views of large Ammonia Compressors in the Derby Works**

Each machine has a pair of horizontal compressors driven by a vertical triple expansion steam engine. This type was supplied to The River Plate Fresh Meat Company

*Picture the Past Derbyshire*

61

**Figure 29. This electrically powered ammonia compression machine was supplied to New Zealand**
*Haslam 1923 Catalogue*

**Figure 30. Belt Driven Ammonia Duplex Machine**
*Haslam 1923 Catalogue*

| Size Range | 4 | 12 |
|---|---|---|
| Refrigerating capacity- tons per 24 hours | 4.5 | 45 |
| Horsepower | 9 | 70 |
| Revs per minute | 400 | 325 |
| Overall Width inches | 28 | 48 |
| Overall Length inches | 58 | 88 |
| Weight cwts | 17 | 61 |

**Figure 31. Large Ammonia Duplex Compressor driven by a 3300 Volt Motor. Supplied to a major Brewery Company**
*Haslam 1923 Catalogue*

**Figure 32. Large four-cylinder enclosed Ammonia Compressor driven by a 250 horse power diesel engine.**
**Supplied for a tropical ice-making Plant producing 50 tons of ice per day**
*Haslam 1923 Catalogue*

**Figure 33. Duplex Carbon Dioxide Refrigerating Machine**
*Haslam 1923 Catalogue*

This integral steam driven machine is fitted with Liquid Cooling Economiser and Multiple Effect Compressors which increases the refrigerating capacity of the machine by 25 to 100% according to the temperature of the condensing water and reduces the power required per ton of refrigeration by 15 to 40%. Features that are particularly useful for marine plants working in tropical conditions. As supplied to Messrs Alfred Holt Ltd; the SS 'Meriones' and the SS 'Sarpendon'.

**Figure 34. Motor Driven Carbon Dioxide Machine**
*Haslam 1923 Catalogue*

This machine has two double acting compressors on a stand containing copper condensing coils. It is driven through gearing by an electric motor. The machine is fitted with a Patent Liquid Cooling economiser.

# 11A

# Special Installations

## Ice Rink

In the early part of the twentieth century an 'out of the ordinary' project was the installation of the machinery for an ice rink in Glasgow, for the sport of curling. The formal opening was reported in The *Derby Daily Telegraph*, December 12, 1907.Two machines of the ammonia compression type provided the refrigeration.

One machine for keeping the rink frozen and the other for making 25 tons of ice per day, or both can work on the rink if necessary. The reason for large amount of ice production is not clear.

The machines were used to cool brine below the freezing point of water; 'the brine being circulated around six miles of iron piping under the ice floor. Over 100 tons of ice constituted the floor measuring 140 feet by 98 feet - the pipes being so arranged that a perfectly even surface is the result.

Sir Charles Dundas declared the rink open and played the first shot. Sir Alfred Haslam was present and received many congratulations on the success of the rink. Following the success of this project other ice rinks, equipped with Haslam machinery, were constructed.

## Air Supply to Blast furnaces

A novel use of refrigeration was the 'Haslam' development for drying air supplies to blast furnaces and steel convertors. Removing moisture from the air supply improved the overall efficiency of the furnace system, for example-saving in the amount of fuel used; a higher temperature in the furnace; an increase in the amount of iron and more regular working of the furnace, plus other advantages.

Drying was achieved by channelling the air through a 'Haslam Patent Air Cooling Battery' system. This comprised a two-section array of pipes through which cold water and brine circulated; electrically powered, ammonia refrigerating machines being used to cool the water and brine.

A brief description of the process was included in the '*Iron, Steel and Allied Trades Souvenir*' publication produced for their 1910 meeting at Buxton, Derbyshire, viz:-

> The battery is divided into two sections. The first is known as the water battery, where cooled water circulates at 35 degrees F. Air is circulated over this battery and cooled to within about 1 degree of the water temperature. The second section known as the brine battery is where brine circulates at a temperature of say 10 degrees F. The air passing over this is further reduced in temperature as required. The air is then channelled to the 'blower' machinery which generates the 'blast' to the furnace'.

**Figure 35. Refrigerating Machinery for drying the air supply to Blast
Furnaces. Capacity - 100,000 cubic ft of air per minute
Supplied to Messrs Alfred Hickman Ltd. (c. 1910)**

*Haslam 1923 Catalogue*

A very large plant at Messr's Alfred Hickman [Figure 35] has the capacity of drying 100,000 cubic feet of air per minute. It was constructed that input air at 90 degrees F containing 8 grains of moisture per cubic foot is discharged from the brine battery at say 20-degree F with 1.2 grains of moisture per cubic foot. The plant has been working for 6 months night and day without a single stoppage or difficulty at any time. The Company are now engaged in erecting a smaller plant at Stanton Iron Works near Nottingham (*Haslam Catalogue*).

.

# Medical Research

The following has been sourced from Haslam family papers and archives of the London School of Hygiene and Tropical Medicine, mainly the Sir Ronald Ross Collection. [Ross/110/02et seq.]*

A novel, experimental use of refrigeration in the second decade of the twentieth century was for research into the effect of cryotherapy (use of low temperatures) on the treatment of tropical diseases.

Apparently, Sir Edwin Durning-Lawrence, baronet, had discussed this type of treatment with Sir Alfred Haslam. Subsequently, Sir Edwin was in contact with the Liverpool school of Tropical Medicine and in February 1909 sent a cheque for £500 to cover the cost of a cold chamber and for refrigeration trials at the school (Sir Edwin also provided more finance as time went on).

In February 1909 the Secretary of the School requested Sir Alfred to advise on the refrigeration equipment. In a letter dated February, 27, 1909, Sir Alfred stated he *'would do very much to assist'*. During May 1909 a diagram [Figure 36] of the refrigerating plant proposed by Haslam's was accepted by the School and subsequently installed. Experiments were begun to discover – the influence, if any, of a cold climate in modifying or preventing the occurrence of certain tropical diseases.

Trials were supervised by Ronald Ross, a British medical doctor who had received the Nobel Prize for Physiology or Medicine in 1902 for his long term investigations to prove the transmission of malaria by mosquitos. Later, in 1911, he had the honour of being knighted.

Initially, trials were carried out on small animals e.g. guinea pigs and rats. However, in a letter to Sir Alfred in April 1910 Ross stated – nothing very definite has been obtained with animals and everyone suggests that we must try and work with a human patient. One human patient – a sleeping sickness case – briefly used it. However, the patient proved unsuitable as the drug being used affected his eyesight.

Attempts were made to find other human patients including approaches to other hospitals but – local doctors were not sending patients for treatment in the cold chamber (letter from Ross to Sir Edwin March, 2, 1911). Ross admitted to Sir Alfred in October 1911 – we entirely failed in getting any human patients to come to the room, the machine having being shut down temporarily during the summer.

Research on animals carried on but, in June 1913 Ross wrote to ask Sir Edwin if he wished the experiments to continue in the face of the local lack of interest. Sir Edwin decided to close down the research and for the refrigeration machine to be sold, Sir Alfred finally buying it back for £30.

*Copyright of the Ross Family, courtesy of the Library and Archives Service, London School of Hygiene & Tropical Medicine

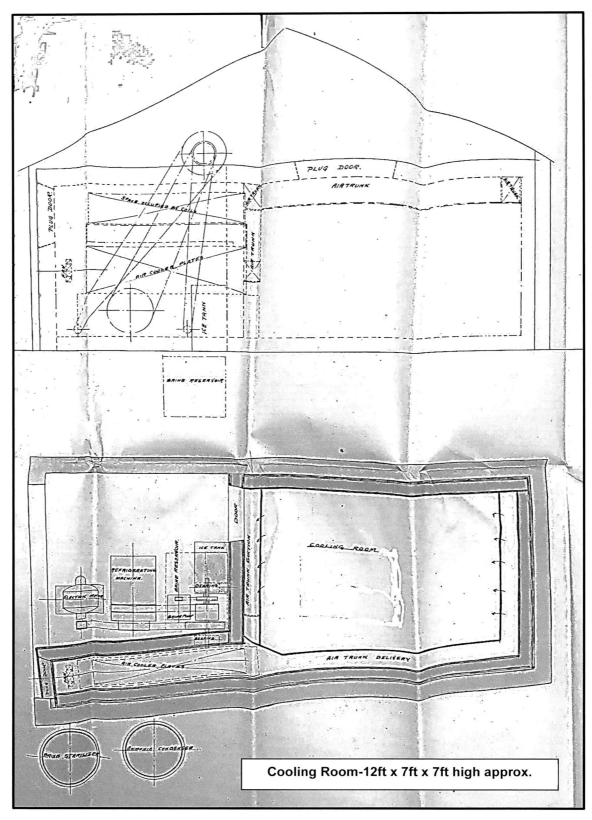

Cooling Room-12ft x 7ft x 7ft high approx.

Figure 36. Medical Research-Proposed Experimental Refrigerating Plant.
Re-produced from Haslam Drawing 6636/221. Dated May 29, 1909
*Copyright of the Haslam family. Courtesy of The Library & Archives Service.*
*London School of Hygiene & Tropical Medicine*

# 12A

# Potential Sale of the Company

There are indications that Alfred was considering the sale of the Company as early as 1909. This thought could well have been influenced by the death of his oldest son Victor during 1907. Victor was a principal of the company and most likely would have succeeded his father in running the business.

A reference to a new company is in correspondence between Alfred and Margaret, the widow of Edmund Pontifex an original shareholder and a director in the Haslam Company. Edmund had died on October 12, 1909, leaving an estate valued at £17,238- 5s-2d. Harriet in reply to a letter of sympathy from Sir Alfred wrote:-

> He often spoke of you to me, and I always understood you were old friends. May I also mention that he has left me by Will 22 Haslam Foundry shares and I do not know what I should do in regard to them? I know what splendid dividends they have always paid and that I shall have to look to them, to form part, and nearly all, of my future income. Would you advise me to sell, and if so, what price I am likely to get for them?

> Will you also kindly tell me, if when you find a successor, which I hope will not be for a very long time, if I should be entered as a shareholder in the new Co. I should be extremely obliged if you will tell me anything concerning the Co.

Going forward to 1917, letters indicate that Alfred, then aged 73, was continuing to look at options for sale of the Company.

A total of 17 letters, dating from September 1917 to February 1918 and then from February 1920 to August 1923, show that he was in discussion with Mr Ward of the firm J & E Hall Ltd, a business rival in refrigeration equipment. Mostly the letters were to Sir Alfred with only a few copy letters in return. Also, they were general in content, so the overall 'picture' is incomplete. The earliest letter, September 23, 1917, refers to a previous letter so when discussions commenced is not clear.

In a letter to Mr Ward, February 18, 1918, Sir Alfred had no objection to accountants from J & E Hall meeting with his accountants but was reluctant to proceed with formal discussions:-

> … because of the large volume of war work which has recently increased which was keeping him fully occupied.

A letter from February 28, 1920, indicated discussions had re-started. During July 1923 the accountants' visit was made. A letter to Sir Alfred dated July 20, 1923, [Appendix E] showed hesitancy by J & E Hall Ltd. Subsequently Mr Ward visited the works. However, the culmination of this was that Mr Ward wrote in the August to say that they were not prepared to make an offer and negotiations ceased.

During the same period other options for a sale were being sought:-

**March 21, 1921** Reply from Vestey Brothers saying they were not interested –

> … in participating in part or wholly in taking over the business you mentioned; because our requirements would be a very small portion of the total output of our Works.

Vestey Brothers were international dealers in the meat trade. They were pioneers in the use of refrigeration and owned a fleet of refrigerated ships and users of refrigeration installations.

**June 1922 to February 1924** Seven letters from a London solicitor, acting on behalf of their Clients Messrs Myers and Co, London re the sale of the Company. Preliminary discussions took place but no further progress was made.

# 13A

# Death of Sir Alfred 1927

## The End of an Era

The family and the Company must have been shocked when they heard the sad news that the now Sir Alfred had died in St Pancras Hotel, London while on a business trip. The date was January 23, 1927. He was 83 years old and the principal shareholder in the business.

Alfred's death marked the end of an era lasting 59 years, during which the Company had grown from small beginnings to a an internationally respected firm producing refrigeration equipment and other products.

National Archive records[16] show that the business became a Private Limited Company in 1908 with the majority of the shares being owned by family members. The distribution of shares in 1922 is shown in the table below.

| Share Holdings for 1922 | |
|---|---|
| Haslam Sir Alfred | 895 |
| Haslam Lady Ann (nee Tatam) | 8 |
| Haslam William G (Brother) | 36 |
| Haslam Susannah (Wife of William G) | 4 |
| Haslam Ethel (a widow) Haslam Eric Seale      Shared Holding (Son of Alfred) | 4 |
| Haslam Gerald Haigh (Son of William G) | 1 |
| Ham Hilda (Married daughter) | 2 |
| Haslam Eric Seale (Son) | 4 |
| Pontifex Mrs (Widow of Edmund Pontifex*) | 44 |
| Tatam Frank (Brother in law) | 2 |
| **Total Shares - nominal value £100 each** | **1000** |
| *One of the original Directors of the Company | |

The Directors of the Company were Alfred and his brother William; only two directors being required to satisfy the new company rules. By far the majority of the shares were held by Sir Alfred. An outcome of his death was the sale of the Company along with properties and financial investments to help settle tax and death duties. Under new owners the business traded for a further 10 years until 1937.

The 1930s was a period of a serious economic downturn both in Britain and internationally. This situation seriously affected trading conditions and the factory closed in 1937 with production being moved to Scotland by the then owners L Sterne and Co. The life cycle of the Company is depicted in Figure 37. Events during the final 10 years are described in Chapter 14A.

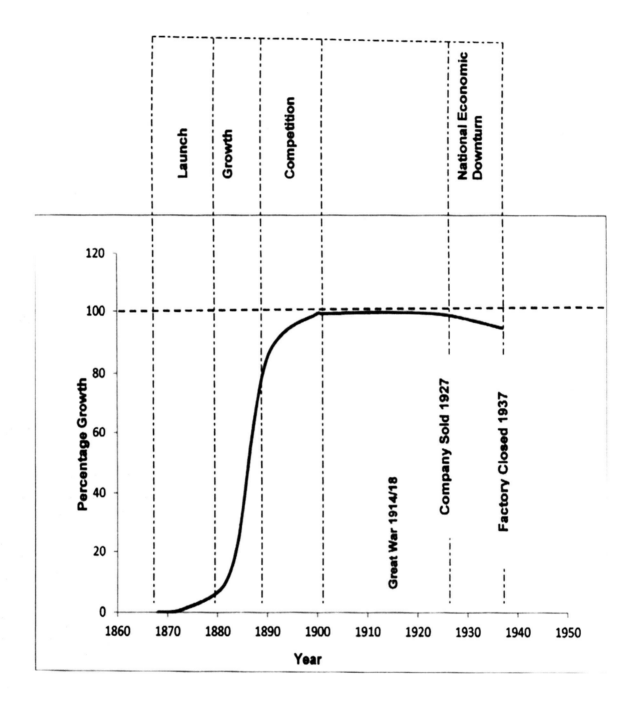

**Figure 37. Life Cycle of the Haslam Company**

# 14A

# The Final Years 1927 to 1939

## 1927 Onwards

An outcome of Sir Alfred's death in January 1927 was the sale of the Company along with his properties and financial investments to help settle tax and death duties. Several Directors and Extraordinary General Meetings (EGM) were held over the next few months[11] . [Appendix F]

**February 15, 1927** - At an EGM of shareholders, chaired by William Gilbert Haslam, a resolution was passed that Eric Seale Haslam (a son of Sir Alfred) be appointed a Director of the Company. It was recorded that:-

> The meeting desired to be put on record their regret at the loss the Company had sustained by the death of Sir Alfred Seale Haslam, Managing Director from its commencement and to express their appreciation of the eminent services rendered by him to the Company for over fifty years.

**March 18** - A meeting of Directors resolved that the Company's investments be sold and put in a special shareholder's bank account.

**June 14** - A Directors' meeting agreed for the sale of the Company and assets to Mr H B Potter, appoint him as Director, and to start the procedures for voluntary liquidation of the Company.

**July 19 -** Agreement for sale of the Company was formally agreed by Directors and Company seal affixed.

**October 13** - At an EGM of shareholders formal proposals for the sale of the Company and its voluntary liquidation were agreed by the meeting. Later, resolutions made at this meeting were confirmed at an EGM on October 28.

An article in the *Derby Daily Telegraph*, August 1, 1927, reported that the purchasers were Mr H Potter, managing director of H B Potter and Co Ltd, Rochdale, asbestos manufacturers and Mr J Lord, Managing Director of Kelsall and Kemp Ltd, Rochdale, flannel and cloth manufacturers.

The *Sheffield Daily Telegraph*, November 11, reported that on November 9, 1927, a new company '**The Haslam Foundry and Engineering Company (1927) Ltd'** was registered; the nominal capital being £175,000 Cumulative Preference shares and 100,000 Ordinary shares at £1 each. Mr Lord was to be Chairman for 5 years. Other directors were Mr Potter (MD); engineer W G Haslam, Derby (*Alfred's brother)*; engineer W R Sharp, London; Accountant, H Clayton, Cheam.

The list of activities was comprehensive: - To carry on the business of manufacturers of machinery of all descriptions, internal combustion and other engines, agricultural, marine, salvage, aero, sanitary, water supply, electrical engineers, boiler makers, brass founders, iron and non-ferrous metal founders, millwrights, builders, electric lighting manufacturers, contractors, motor cars, omnibuses etc. Strangely, refrigeration was not listed.

# Haslam and Newton Ltd

The '1927' version of Haslam's (above) was an interim situation because only eleven months later the *Derby Daily Telegraph* [October 5, 1928] reported that Haslam Foundry and Engineering Company (1927) Ltd and Newton Brothers Ltd had agreed to join forces. Newton Brothers Ltd was a long-established electrical engineering firm on Alfreton Road, Derby. This, apparently, was part of a scheme to develop artificial silk production facilities.

The formal amalgamation was announced on October 20; the title of the company being Haslam and Newton Ltd. Several newspapers published the abridged prospectus for the Company, for example the '*Yorkshire Post and Leeds Intelligence*' on October 24, 1928.

The Directors were:-

> Mr. J H Lord, Chairman, Haslam Foundry & Engineering Company (1927) Ltd
> Mr. W G Haslam, Director, Haslam Foundry & Engineering Company (1927) Ltd
> Mr. C A Newton, Director, Newton Brothers (Derby) Ltd
> Lt Col H Newton, Director, Newton Brothers (Derby) Ltd
> G J Teunissen, (Dutch) Berkheide, Rijksdporp Holland, Continental Representative
> Mr. H B Potter, Managing Director, Haslam Foundry & Engineering Co. (1927) Ltd
> Mr. F Newton, Managing Director, Newton Brothers (Derby) Ltd
> Mr. J H Lord was Chairman of the Company, and Mr. H B Potter, together with Mr. Fred Newton acted as Joint managing directors, to ensure management continuity.

The Company Prospectus (Figure 38) states that one of Haslam's specialities was the manufacture of artificial silk plants of all types and that Newton's manufactured the electrical systems. The Prospectus stated that the new company:- will now be in a position to contract for the complete equipment of spinning and weaving plants for the production of artificial silk, which has not hitherto been possible.

Only a month after the formation of Haslam and Newton Ltd, the *Sheffield Daily Telegraph* [November 5, 1928] reported the formation of the British Netherlands Artificial Silk Company Ltd. The Company having the objective of developing two artificial silk factories, one in an existing building in Wigton, Cumberland plus an intention to develop a factory at a site in Deadman's Lane Derby. The Directors appointed included several from Haslam and Newton Ltd along with Dutch partners who had the expertise for artificial silk manufacture Contracts for manufacture of some of the equipment, was awarded to Haslam and Newton Ltd. The site at Wigton was fitted out by 1930. However, it was never operated, [Figures 39 & 40]. The factory was put up for sale in 1931 - due to the depressed state of the artificial silk business at home and abroad.

**(Figure 38) HASLAM AND NEWTON LTD ABRIDGED PROSPECTUS**
Extracts[12]

The Company has been incorporated particularly for the purpose of taking over the businesses of the Haslam Foundry and Engineering Company (1927) Ltd and Newton Bros (Derby) Ltd. These two well-known engineering companies have a worldwide reputation and are both in Derby.

THE HASLAM FOUNDRY AND ENGINEERING COMPANY (1927) LIMITED

The business was founded by the late Sir Alfred Seale Haslam in 1868 as a general engineering business, and in 1876 was converted into the Haslam Foundry and Engineering Co. Ltd. It was the pioneer in the manufacture of cold-air refrigerating machinery, and the first cargoes of frozen meal imported on a commercial basis were brought to this country on ships fitted with Haslam machines.

Since that time there has been extensive development in the manufacture of machines on the ammonia and carbonic anhydride systems for both land and marine work, and the firm has become one of the leading makers of refrigerating machinery, its products being in use all over the world.

The Company specialises in the manufacture of artificial silk plant of all types, chemical plant, distillation plant, etc., and includes among its customers the largest artificial silk and chemical manufacturing Companies in the United Kingdom, and also many of the leading cold and produce companies. It has recently supplied machinery to the Orient Company for their new liner Orford, and has installed plant on four of the new ships of the Blue Star Line. The uses to which refrigerating plant can be applied are increasing extensively, and the business is well equipped to supply a large proportion of the demand for such plant.

NEWTON BROTHERS (DERBY) LIMITED

The business was established in the year 1899 and is one of the most successful electrical engineering manufacturers in this country. By reason of the extremely valuable patents which it owns, it is in a position to secure a large amount of specialised electrical engineering work. It is common knowledge that the demand for electrical equipment during the next few years will be on a much greater scale than in the past.

Its customers include many Government departments, both at home and abroad, and it has representation throughout the world. The electrical power equipment for a large number of the wireless stations and for many of the telephone exchanges in this country has been manufactured by the Newton Company, which also manufactures electrical equipment for the artificial silk, weaving, and spinning industries.

**Figure 39. Refrigerator Compressor**
**Wigton**
*Haslam & Newton Photo*

**Figure 40. Steeping Presses**
**Wigton**
*Haslam & Newton Photo*

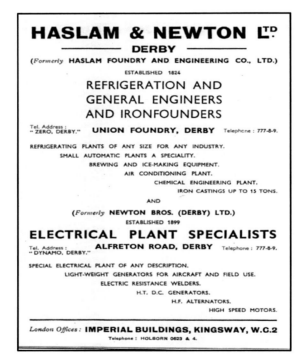

**Figure 41. Haslam & Newton Ltd**
*Picture the Past Derbyshire*

The advertisement [Figure 41] shows a wide range of engineering capabilities. Refrigeration remained the main business for the Haslam side of the Company. For example, in 1930, they supplied machinery for a Derby Co-operative Society abattoir in Woods Lane. Then in 1931 refrigerating equipment was installed at a new ice rink in Southampton and then at Earls Court, the largest one in Europe.

However, newspaper reports of the Company's annual meetings indicated that trade and profits were erratic with 1932 being the worst loss experienced by the

Company; blame being put on the national economic situation. At the AGM in July 1933 the Chairman stated that the Company had turned the corner with no loss but little profit. However, in 1935 the Company split back to the two individual companies.

# L Sterne and Co Ltd

In January 1935, the *Aberdeen Press and Journal* reported that the well-established Messrs L Sterne and Co Ltd, refrigerating engineers of Glasgow had acquired controlling interest in the refrigeration activities of the Haslam Company. The Haslam and Newton Ltd company was dissolved and a sale of the refrigeration undertaking was made to a new company with the original name of Haslam Foundry and Engineering Co Ltd with L Sterne and Co Ltd directing the future control and policy. This arrangement was formalized in April 1935 with the 'Newton' side of the business reverting to Newton Bros (Derby) Ltd during May.

This extract from *A History of the 'Sterne' Company*\*, written by the then Chairman Sir Samuel R Beale, gives background information on the events:-

> In 1935 we completed the negotiations for the acquisition of the Haslam Foundry & Engineering Company at Derby including their marine and Admiralty contracts.
>
> We had been approached by Mr Cooper Parry, a well-known Chartered Accountant in Derby. Apparently over-capitalisation and bad trade by Haslam and Newton had got them into the hands of the bank, on whose behalf they were offered to us. The final arrangement, given in the Directors' Report for 1935, was:
>
> Early this year the Directors concluded an arrangement by which the Company secured control of the refrigerating machinery business of Messrs. Haslam & Newton, Ltd. of Derby. A new Company, reverting to the old name of the Haslam Foundry and Engineering Co. Ltd. has been formed to acquire these assets. The purchase price of 77 per cent of the shares of this new Company was £8,ooo in cash and 5834 ordinary shares of the Company.
>
> Our idea in acquiring this business was really two-fold. We wanted their marine connections, and more manufacturing capacity. However, the technique of running two works so far apart, and with quite different traditions, defeated us, but we gained a good deal of knowledge, and I have never regretted the policy. After this purchase our marine business became seriously substantial,

On October 29, 1937, *The Scotsman* reported that L Sterne and Co Ltd had decided to transfer the business to Glasgow. The reason given was that they had found it impossible to continue profitable manufacture in Derby.

It is most likely that during transfer of the business to Glasgow drawings and records were either destroyed or taken to Scotland. L Sterne and Co continued to manufacture 'Haslam' machinery for some years.

\*University of Glasgow, Archives and Special Collections

# Thos. W Ward (Ltd) Sheffield

The *Derby Daily Telegraph* on November 3, 1937, reported that the works and plant but not the good will had been purchased by Thos. W Ward (Ltd) Sheffield. The firm was a used machinery and plant merchant.

The press report described that the factory covered an area of around five acres, complete with fully equipped engineering shops plus iron and non-ferrous foundries. The plant included a good number of first-class machine tools with the whole being a very desirable type of engineering works ready for immediate operation. The purchasers said no decision had been reached on the future of the works but they were open to proposals for acquisition of the property as a general engineering concern. It is not known what, or if any, plant and machinery was disposed of by Thos. Ward before they sold the factory.

# E W Bliss Ltd

On August 17, 1939, The *Derby Daily Telegraph* reported that E W Bliss Ltd had purchased the factory. Extensive structural alterations were to be started immediately. E W Bliss Ltd was an American based firm specializing in various types of presses, large power presses, hydraulic presses and other machinery.

# Observations on the 'The Final Years'

At the time of Sir Alfred's death, in January 1927, the directors of the Company were Sir Alfred and his brother William Gilbert, two directors then being the number required by the Company rules. Hence, after Alfred's death, at the February 1927 EGM, Eric, Alfred's son, was formally named as the second director with William Gilbert being the senior director.

Only four months later, in June, a decision was made to sell the Company to Mr H B Potter (and his colleague Mr J Lord). There was no suggestion that other potential buyers had been approached. Most likely, therefore, Potter and Lord had been negotiating for a purchase before Alfred's death.

The purchase and subsequent formation of the '1927' version of the Haslam Company followed only a year later by the creation of Haslam and Newton Ltd apparently was a scheme to provide facilities for the manufacture of equipment for the production of artificial silk. In the same period the British Netherlands Artificial Silk Company Ltd was formed to manufacture artificial silk, the Board of Directors including several from Haslam and Newton Ltd. As mentioned previously, a factory was fitted out but never went into production due to poor 'market conditions.

The final years of the 'Haslam' Factory from 1927 to 1937 were during a period of a severe national economic downturn, a 'knock-on' effect of a global 'Great Depression'. This situation seriously affected industrial areas and would have been a reason for Haslam and Newton Ltd and then L Sterne and Co have cause to reorganise. As Alfred conceived it, the surviving building of his works still (2020) acts as a backdrop to Chester Green.

# 15A

# Farnborough Cold Air Machine

## 1935 to 1977

From 1928 to 1937 the factory was run first by Haslam & Newton Ltd then later by L Sterne and Co. The photograph in Figure 42 dated 1935-36, shows a dry air machine with text saying it was for the Air Ministry at South Farnborough. Enquiries made to 'Farnborough Air Sciences Trust' (FAST) created much interest and resulted in the following detailed information being received from Mr Cooper, a retired engineer[9].

> The Haslam cold air machine was installed in the engine test bay at the Royal Aircraft Establishment (RAE), Farnborough, in the mid 1930s. Its object was to provide cold air for the altitude testing facilities of aero engines. It served this purpose for the next 10 years when it was superseded by similar equipment obtained through Operation Surgeon. Surgeon was the recovery of interesting engineering plant and equipment as war-time reparation from Germany. The Haslam machine was retained for possible future use elsewhere.

> In the mid 1940s RAE required a high-altitude test facility for aircraft alternators; such equipment being used in aircraft electrics to replace the 24-volt direct current generators. This new facility was given the name of Generator Test House (GTH). It was for this facility that the Haslam machine was brought back into use.

> The machine basically was a vertical, reciprocating, medium speed air compressor with two cylinders above each connecting-rod. I think the upper cylinders were used as compressors; the air being delivered through a cooler into the lower cylinders which acted as expanders. Delivery from the machine was cold air due to adiabatic expansion. Due to recovery of power from the expansion cylinders the machine appeared to be driven by a ridiculously small electric motor.

> In the GTH installation the air inlet to the compressor was supercharged by air from a Hick-Hargreaves rotary compressor delivering air through a drying bed of activated alumina. The cold air output from the Haslam machine was routed through the test chambers as dry, cold air under low pressure by a series of exhausters.

Mr Cooper was present, as a young engineer, during the commissioning of the new GTH facility and commented that:-

> On commissioning the plant, it was interesting to see the Haslam machine 'freewheeling' by virtue of the booster compressor alone. It was a pleasure to see the Mr Haslam of that time, with pipe in mouth, appearing delighted with extreme satisfaction at seeing his beloved machine working again in its new surroundings. The relevant date would be about 1947. The GTH plant was demolished in 1977 to allow passage to the new RAE entrance from Pinehurst Avenue.

**Figure 42. Haslam & Newton Dry Air Machine built for the Air Ministry
at South Farnborough -1935-36.
Final Testing at the Derby works**
*Picture the Past Derbyshire*

The 'Mr Haslam' mentioned in the 1947 trials must have been Gerald Haigh Haslam - a nephew of Sir Alfred. He had been employed at the factory, in different roles, for his entire career. He was born in 1886 so would have been around 60 years old during the trials. At that date, presumably, personnel from L Sterne and Co were commissioning the machine with Gerald Haslam acting in a consultancy role.

# Derby Ice Factory

## 1899 to 1975

In January 1899 several local newspapers reported on a proposed ice factory in Derby:-

> We are glad to report the public that definite arrangements have been made to establish an Ice Factory and Cold Storage Rooms in the town. The enterprise has been energetically taken up by Henry Bemrose, Sir Alfred Haslam and other influential gentlemen. A site has been secured at the canal wharf in Siddals Road …… It will have a frontage on the road.

**Ice Factory c. 1970**

On the ground floor would be the general office; the refrigerating machines along with the boilers to power the machinery and, three chill rooms for freshly killed meat.

On the first floor would be an ice making machine able to make 5 tons of ice per 24 hours plus a store room for the ice to meet the variable demands of the trade. There also would be a room for general storage of frozen meat, butter, cheese, poultry, eggs etc. The second floor would have a large store used for the storage of hops for use by local brewers. A third floor will be insulated and used as demand for storage is required.

A lift would serve all floors and the building would have electric lighting throughout. Refrigeration was to be of the ammonia compression type. The ammonia refrigerant circulating around an array of corrugated pipes called a 'battery' patented by Sir Alfred Haslam. By means of a fan cold air is produced by passing it through the battery; the air is then circulated around the cold rooms as required.

The building is convenient to the abattoirs in the cattle market and being central will be useful for tradesmen who wish to store perishable goods, for example - butchers, hotels, fishmongers, provision merchants etc. The report concluded:-

> … In the meantime, Messrs Haslam is busily engaged in the manufacture of the necessary machinery.

Originally the company's name was 'The Pure Derby Ice and Cold Storage Company' as part of the 'Haslam Engineering and Foundry Company Ltd'. In 1921 The *Nottingham Journal* reported that a new limited company 'The Derby Pure Ice and Storage Company Ltd' had been formed to take over the business. The directors were named as Sir Alfred Haslam, W G Haslam (brother), E S Haslam (son) and G H Haslam (nephew).

An advertisement by the Company [Figure 43] shows that sales included eggs and salt in various forms. Apparently, sales of salt were significant enough for a special warehouse to be built.

## Derby Pure Ice & Cold Storage Co., Ltd.

### PURE ICE

made from Town Water, delivered to all parts of the town and district.

### COLD STORAGE

for all purposes, in large or small consignments. The ordinary householder catered for.

### ICE REFRIGERATORS

for Trade or Household purposes. Call and inspect our Stock. Prices from £3, with guaranteed deliveries of Ice.

### NEW LAID EGGS

Wholesale Merchants.   All eggs tested and guaranteed.
THE TRADE SUPPLIED.

### CHILLED EGGS

Proprietors of the celebrated " Polar " Brand. Largely increased supplies will be available during next winter.

### SALT

for all purposes. Agricultural, Bar, Rock, Freezing, etc.

Further information from—

D. R. PILLING,

Manager

MORLEDGE, DERBY.

**Figure 43. Derby Ice Factory Advert 1930**

**Salt Warehouse**
*K Reedman*

The original refrigerating machines were of the ammonia compression type powered by steam from coal-fired boilers, coal being transported along the canal and cooling water for the condensers being taken from the canal. Later, the machinery was updated and powered electrically.

The company remained in business well into the twentieth century. Finally, it was purchased by the Derby Council during, the 1970s, for demolition, to allow building development and highway improvements. Soon before demolition began the building was gutted by fire in July 1975.

# Part B

# Sir Alfred and Family

**Lady Ann Haslam**

**Sir Alfred Haslam**

**William Gilbert Haslam
Brother**

**Alfred Victor Haslam**

**William Kenneth Haslam**

**Eric Haslam**

**Hilda Haslam**

**Edith Haslam**

# Sir Alfred and Family

# Preface

These chapters cover the personal lives and experiences of Alfred and his family made possible by the income and share dividends generated by his highly successful company. The trading life of the Company is described in Part A. For continuity main points are outlined below and elsewhere in subsequent chapters.

During mid-Victorian times discussions were being held in and out of Parliament of how to meet the growing demand for meat in Britain. On the other hand, in Australia for example, there was a surplus of mutton as sheep were bred mainly for wool production. Hence, a commercial incentive existed to discover a feasible method of shipping this surplus meat without being spoiled.

Refrigeration was an evolving technology. Ships fitted with refrigeration systems for storing frozen carcases would be the solution. Alfred would have been aware of this commercial opportunity. In 1873, he was the head of a successful engineering business at the Union Foundry in Derby. This provided the facilities for him to begin designing and developing refrigeration machinery.

As well as Alfred, other firms were pursuing the same ends, the Bell-Coleman Mechanical Refrigeration Company being the main rival. The method considered most suitable for on-board use was the 'cold air' system. To produce the freezing effect cold air was generated and circulated around the cold storage chambers.

Two ships fitted with Bell-Coleman machinery, carrying frozen cargos, arrived in Britain from Australia during February 1880 and September 1881. Alfred was not far behind. Three ships of the Orient shipping line fitted with 'Haslam' machines successfully completed voyages arriving in Britain during October and November 1881. Following the success of these voyages the Orient Line fitted Haslam machinery to all their ships so creating the first shipping line to go into the frozen meat trade on a regular basis.

For a period both firms were supplying machines. Rivalry arose and legal actions were taken over patent infringements. Alfred, c. 1884, settled the dispute by buying the patents and the manufacturing rights from Bell-Coleman. From then on, the Haslam business 'took off'. For the next 10 years or so Haslam machines virtually 'cornered' the market for marine refrigeration installations plus many land installations in Britain and abroad. To cope with the demand the Union Foundry factory was extended in stages, the workforce numbers increasing likewise.

During the 1890s, there was growing competition to the cold air machines. Other more efficient machines, had been developed. To match this competition the Haslam Company, over several years, developed these types of machines resulting in cold air machines to gradually cease production. The Company continued trading profitably until 1927 when it was sold following the death of Alfred.

# 1B

# Formative Years

Alfred Seale Haslam was born in Derby in the early years of Queen Victoria's reign, on the October 27, 1844[1], and grew up at a time when the town was in the forefront of industrial experiment and innovation. He was the fourth of five sons plus three daughters born to William and Anne Haslam.

His father, William Haslam, was a bronze and black smith, working in Belper until his marriage in 1838 to Anne, the daughter of Joseph Smith of Branston, near Burton on Trent in Staffordshire, About this time they moved to Derby where William took over an established business and showroom at 2-3, St Helen's Street[1] on the north side of Derby, and here he set himself up as a brass founder, bell hanger and smith, employing four workmen[2]. The family home and workshop were further down the street.

| Alfred's Parents and Family | |
|---|---|
| **Parents** | |
| William Haslam | 1805-1878 |
| Married | 1838 |
| Ann Smith | 1812-1879 |
| **Family** | |
| John | 1839-1917 |
| William | 1841-1851 |
| Edwin | 1843-1913 |
| Alfred Seale | 1844-1927 |
| Annie Hannah | 1848-1871 |
| Mary Maria | 1850-1930 |
| Martha Louise | 1853-1916 |
| William Gilbert | 1855-1935 |

**Showroom, St Helen's Street**

William was a highly skilled craftsman. When the Great Exhibition at the Crystal Palace took place in 1851, William submitted a great chapel door embellished with wrought iron scrollwork. As an example of the style of ancient church iron work it won much praise and a prize medal. It became a family heirloom and was eventually placed in Alfred's care, it can be seen at Breadsall Priory, near Derby. The advertisement shows commendations made for the door and the wide range of products produced by William Haslam.

WILLIAM HASLAM, BELL HANGER, BRASS FOUNDER, AND SMITH. ST HELEN'S STREET, DERBY

Brass plates, Rods, Tubes and Castings to order. Old brass work restored. Ornamental wrought-iron Grates, Palisades, Screens, etc. to suit the various styles of Architecture. Wrought-iron work for: - churches, scroll hinges, locks, vanes etc.

A specimen of Church Iron Work Shown by William Haslam at the Great Exhibition of 1851 received an unsolicited illustration in the "Art Journal Catalogue," and "The Builder", and also a prize medal from the "Art Journal Catalogue". This attempt on the part of Mr. Haslam to imitate the style of the Ancient Church wrought-iron work, which was carried to such high perfection in the thirteenth century, has been eminently successful. *Taken from Freebody, Directory of Derby 1852.*

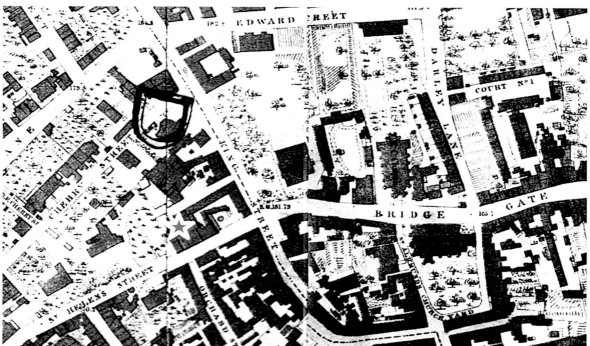

The map, taken from the 1852 Board of Health Map, shows the Haslam home in St Helen's Street, marked with a star. Bridge Gate is shown running down to the River Derwent.

Alfred's parents were General Baptists, a minority church within Derby's large nonconformist population. When William settled in St. Helen's Street the family would have worshipped at a small chapel on Brook Street, just a few hundred yards from their home. Here, the minister was Reverend John Gregory Deodatus

Pike (1784-1854), a charismatic preacher who was chosen by the congregation in 1810 and remained pastor until his death. As his congregation grew, a larger building was needed and having expanded Brook Street three times, in 1842 they moved to St Mary's Gate, converting a gentleman's town house into a chapel. The Haslam family would have been part of this move.

The chapel on St. Mary's Gate was large, a religious census held in 1851 recorded that it could seat over 1,000 worshippers. It was also very well supported; the evening congregation regularly exceeded 700 persons[4]. There were two Sunday schools where the Haslam children would doubtless has received their primary education in Bible reading.

As a Baptist, Alfred would have grown up in a Christian household which held that Christ died for all and with a belief in Free Will, that human beings could shape their own destiny. It was not an easy faith as Baptists were required to undertake a solemn covenant which would govern their lives and influence their behaviour. Sunday was a holy day when no work was undertaken, not even the cleaning of a knife or a shoe, and Christmas was a day of devotion, not of feasting and merriment. Baptists were instructed not to enter into debts beyond their means, not to dress extravagantly and to abstain from amusements such as wakes, races, dances, playhouses, cards and frivolous reading.

Reverend Pike had a particular concern for the young and the first of many spiritual books he wrote was 'A Catechism of Scriptural Instructions for Young People', followed by - 'Persuasive to Early Piety'. This would be essential reading for the Haslam children and shaped their formative years[5]. When Reverend Pike died in September 1854, William Haslam was one of the under bearers who carried the coffin in funeral procession through streets thronged with mourners, to Uttoxeter Road cemetery on the south side of Derby[6].

John, the eldest child, was inspired by his upbringing and determined to becomea Baptist minister. In 1859 he entered a Baptist Academy at Rawdon in Yorkshire. Two years later he became pastor of Gildersome Baptist church in Yorkshire, his father being present at his induction[7].

The second child, William, died aged ten so it was Edwin who was destined to follow his father in the family business. Anne Hannah, the eldest daughter, married William Jackson in 1870, Martha Louisa married George Brigden in 1873 and Mary Maria married Henry Buckley in 1874.

The two brothers Alfred and William Gilbert were both inclined towards careers in engineering.

# 2B

# Alfred's Early Career

Alfred opted for an apprenticeship at the Midland Railway works in Derby, *'acquiring a thorough acquaintance with the most practical forms of engineering'*[8]. On completing his railway apprenticeship, he found employment at Allsopp & Sons, a brewery in Burton upon Trent. Four letters from his father chart Alfred's movements in 1867-1868[9]. The first, addressed to him at Allsopps' brewery, shows that Alfred was ready to move on to work for 'Sir W Armstrong'.

---

**Sir William George Armstrong** (1810-1900) - British industrialist and engineer. Initially he worked for eleven years as a solicitor, but took great interest in engineering. He left his law practice in 1847 and founded a works at Elswick-on-Tyne to build hydraulically powered machinery so that cranes hoists, capstans, turntables, and dock gates etc. could be worked in almost any situation. He next improved ordnance for the army and revolutionized the design and manufacture of guns. Armstrong was elected a fellow of the Royal Society in 1843 and in 1859 he was appointed government engineer and superintendent of the royal gun factory at Woolwich. In its heyday, the Elswick factory employed over 25,000 people in the manufacture of hydraulic cranes, ships, locomotives and armaments. He was knighted in 1859 and created a baron in 1887.

---

March 12, 1867

Dear Alfred

I think you are doing pretty well at Burton having comfortable lodgings and means of improvement in the evenings which you may not have in a new place. Still if you mind to move be sure and behave with honour, take no advantage what you sow you may expect to reap. I am not surprised that you should look out for improvement, but as you have had a good place, show some gratitude by behaving well at leaving.

I don't know anything respecting Sir W. Armstrong or his Engineer, but if you join them, I hope you will find them honourable men. But in this matter as in all others make it a matter of prayer, ask for divine guidance. We are short sighted, and know not what a day may bring forth - without God's blessing we cannot be safe for a moment, we cannot prosper; I hope you will seek for, and enjoy this blessing and guidance, you will need it more than ever as years roll on, and as you are exposed to new temptations. Yours affectionately WH

April 3, 1867

Dear Alfred

We were much pleased to receive your letter it did not get here by Morning post, which disappointed us. Mother began to think some evil had befallen you by road or rail we are thankful that God has protected you. You say difficulties presented themselves on every hand and side. We were sorry to hear that, but it gave us much pleasure to find they did not stop your progress. Perhaps you will give us a few details of these obstacles, and let us know what sort of folks you are thrown amongst by this change. We were glad to hear that you got a comfortable room. Is there a good Mechanics Institution? or reading room? near you. They have a very good one at the Sunday School Union and an excellent library, but perhaps that is too far off 56, Old Bailey London EC If you can I should like you to join them for 1 Quarter The expense is light, and they have great variety of reading all the best newspapers & c. I am very busy and have not time for more in fact it is to you we must look for news, you must send three letters to our one, and let them be long ones as London is a wonderful place you have much to describe and send particulars about, especially about Sir W. Armstrong's works and progress. Yours affectionately W. Haslam

PS I don't know whether the address you have given us be correct Penton Terrace I cannot find it London Postal Guide. I shall send a Derby paper if there be anything particular before long

Working for Armstrong's would have introduced Alfred to new types of engineering but his father's next letter, written on April 6, tells us that he wished to leave.

April 6, 1867

Dear Alfred

… I was rather taken by surprise when you expressed a wish to leave Armstrong's so soon as I thought it a first class place for improvement, still money is an object to a young man who would like to be in business by & by Mr Milward and yourself will be better able to judge than I can, whether you are likely to obtain the place if you apply; and to give satisfaction if you get it - you may of course depend upon the influence of myself and friends if it be needed, but I hope your own fitness for the place will do more than my influence, or I should not advise you to try for it - you speak of a letter to Mr Bass I think that would be premature until you have made matters right with Mr Canning:- if he approves of you I think all the rest will be easy. Let me know how you succeed with him. I send Mr Bass's address below, but I should not advise you to call upon him without the consent of Mr Canning. Your letter to John we send on to Atherstone, as they are now at Mr Wiln's. Annie will write and give you all the news. Affectionately yours WH

Who the named persons were is not known? Annie is likely to refer to his eldest sister.

During the following months, Alfred in letters to his father must have been considering starting up his own business. A fourth letter from his father, written 11 months later (March 12, 1868), gave sale details of the Union Foundry situated in Chester Green, Derby. Initially, the letter brings a reprimand from his father for failing to write for a long time but then adds:-

I have been thinking you are not acting very kindly towards me. It is a long time since I had a letter from you. I send you advertisements of the sale of premises and Foundry late "Fox brothers". The Foundry is a good opening for anyone who thoroughly understands the business, but I do not think tool making at Derby has been a very good trade of late some years ago it was a first class affair, but other towns of late taken the lead I think Foxes were behind the times, and the great flatness of trade has given the finishing stroke, and perhaps there has been a want of economy. If you were ready to begin the foundry seems a good choice that is if you had a knowledge of the details of the business, but I fear it would be too great and too speculative an undertaking under present circumstances.

The doubt expressed in the last sentence of the letter did not stop the foundry being purchased and in the ownership of the Haslam family by May 1868, the purchase made possible using a loan from Joseph Smith, an uncle. Hence by July 4, 1868, Alfred aged 24, in partnership with his father William Haslam, as managing Director had set up in business trading as – 'Alfred Seale Haslam and Co' making castings of every description for engineers, millwrights, builders, cast-iron pumps, cheese presses etc. The foundry was situated in City Road, Little Chester (now Chester Green), Derby.

The first aim was to build up the customer base and repay the loan. Alfred now had a base from which to realise his ambitions. The workforce was small of around 20 people but he had his father's name, reputation and experience to support him. It may be that Alfred's marketing ability came to the fore, as by profitable trading, the loan was repaid within five years.

Subsequently, on February 11, 1873, the partnership was formally dissolved by mutual consent with Alfred becoming the Managing Director[14].

However, only a month later, Late in the evening, a fire broke out at the foundry. Fortunately, lack of wind, the rapid arrival of the fire service and Alfred's quick thinking prevented the fire from spreading. The news was widely reported in the press and his brother John, reading it in the local newspaper, was greatly upset. He scrawled a letter and sent it post haste:-

February 18, 1873

> My dear Brother. I was coming this morning from Wood Hall where I have been a day – having had to lecture last night and read in the paper the account of your sad catastrophe. I feel in the moment paralysed. Then I thought I would at once start for Derby but afterwards I felt I must come on here. I don't know whether I shall be able to rest without running over to see you all. I am so dreadfully apprehensive as to the effect it will have on father and mother God help them. I pray. I have a wedding at Huddersfield tomorrow morning else I should start for Derby by first train...[13].

John's concerns were needless. With the help of an insurance pay out, recovery was rapid.

Alfred's father William retired in 1874 and moved to live at Flamstead Terrace, 28, North Street on the Strutt's Park Estate, Derby. He died here on April 21, 1878, at the age of 73. His four sons acted as joint executors to administer an estate valued at around £3,000, Edwin inheriting his father's business. William's widow, Ann, died soon after in 1879. Sadly, his parents would not live to see Alfred's future great success. There is no doubt he was a 'guiding light' in Alfred's early career.

# 3B

# Marriage, Company Growth and Prosperity

| Alfred and Family | |
| --- | --- |
| **Parents** | |
| Alfred S Haslam | 1844-1927 |
| Married 1875 | |
| Hannah Tatam | 1852-1924 |
| **Family** | |
| Alfred Victor | 1876-1907 |
| Hilda Annie | 1878-1958 |
| Edith Hannah | 1882-1941 |
| Eric Seale | 1886-1967 |
| Sybil Geraldine | 1889-1890 |
| William Kenneth | 1893-1917 |

The 1871 census recorded Alfred as still living in the parental home on St Helen's Street. He later removed to 34, Duffield Road[16] [18] perhaps in anticipation of his marriage to Ann Tatam, the elder daughter of farmer Thomas and Mary Tatam of The Elms, Little Eaton. Ann, usually called Annie by her family, was 23 years old to Alfred's 30 years. The marriage took place at the parish church of St Paul in Little Eaton on June 17, 1875, and at first, they lived at 34, Duffield Road. By the 1881 census they had two children - Alfred Victor in 1876, Hilda in 1879, and employed a general servant and a kitchen maid.

During 1876, a limited company named the 'Haslam Foundry and Engineering Co Ltd' was created. Alfred now 32 years of age was named as the Managing Director and principal shareholder plus five shareholding directors. These were engineers and business men who would have provided much experience, credibility and financial support for Alfred.

The main objective of the Company was to produce refrigeration machinery to install in 'freezing works' and on ships for transporting frozen goods over the seas, particularly to help meet the national concern about the shortage of meat. A cold air machine was displayed at an exhibition in Sydney during 1879-80 and a machine had been manufactured and was en route to Australia early in 1881 for a land based freezing works. Successful voyages from Australia to Britain by ships fitted with Haslam machines were made during October and November 1881.

Business and profits grew rapidly, particularly after the takeover of the Bell Coleman activities. Alfred's fortune and status grew resulting in rising family wealth. A new home was built on Duffield Road and about 1885, they moved in. This was North Lees, no 138. It was a large house, with four reception rooms and six bedrooms, but it reflected Alfred's increasing wealth, his ambition and his growing family. The 1891 Census recorded that a nurse and cook had been added to the staff in addition to the existing general servant and kitchen maid.

**North Lees House, October 2019**
*Joan D'Arcy*

Alfred purchased a large plot of land on Duffield Road known then as 'The West Bank and Northlees Estate'. His house 'North Lees' was built on a portion of the estate fronting the West side of Duffield Road, Derby. There have several occupants since Alfred's time, beginning with his brother William.

Currently (2019) it is occupied by the Kingfisher Nursery School. It is a three gabled house facing the road, with a central porch. The architectural style can be described as Victorian Jacobean. The architect is not known; it may have been Fryer or F. C. Coulthurst who designed other buildings for Alfred.

The house interior was lavishly furnished and adorned. The dining room was half lined with oak panelling. This was later removed to Breadsall Priory, the future family home, although a stained-glass window was left behind.

In the event, Alfred and Ann had six children. As mentioned earlier, by the 1881 census Alfred Victor and Hilda Annie had been born. Then two more children were born, Edith Hannah in 1882 and Eric Seale in 1886. Later, during 1893 another son William Kenneth was born.

Another daughter, Sybil Geraldine arrived in 1889 but sadly died at one year old. In the early 1890s, plans were being made to rebuild St Werburgh's Church, Derby to increase its capacity for worshippers (it could seat 800). Sir Alfred donated money for the rebuilding including an offer of a stained-glass window in memory of Sybil. This took place four years after Sybil's death. [*Derbyshire Advertiser* June 29, 1894]

Consecration of the church took place on June 28, 1894. This was a formal occasion; the church was packed including the Mayor, Corporation and many local notables including Sir Alfred and family. Apparently, it was very sunny which lit up the new windows. One in the South aisle was the gift of Sir Alfred and Lady Haslam. In the right-hand corner is written - *In loving memory of Sybil Geraldine, their daughter, Sir Alfred and Lady Seale Haslam dedicate this window 1894.*

Until the mid 1890s the Haslam Company virtually 'cornered' the market for marine refrigeration installations, plus land installations at home and abroad. Ships fitted with Haslam cold air systems were regularly shipping frozen cargos of mutton and beef to Britain, initially from Australia, then New Zealand and South America. In 1881, meat carcases totalled 17,275 while 9 years later in 1890 the annual total had increased to 2,895,294[19]. On the outward voyages the ships carried varied cargos of manufactured goods e.g. linens, calicos, cutlery, tools etc. along with frozen goods for example, fish, game etc. In addition, perishable cargos such as apples and other fruits were successfully transported across the world.

To be capable of meeting the sales demands the workforce steadily increased and the factory extended. The original Union foundry was demolished, more land was purchased and new buildings erected. This occurred in stages over several years. The takeover in 1892 of a long-established London firm of Pontifex and Wood Ltd also increased the workforce and a wide range of products were manufactured. By the mid 1890s the factory covered an area of around five acres.

At the start of the original company in 1868 the workforce was stated as 15 men plus boys, in 1890 during a speech to his workforce Alfred quoted 462 people plus staff at various ports. Then in 1898 the report of a visit made by the Institution of Mechanical Engineers stated that between 600 and 700 people were employed.

In 1876-77 at the formation of the Limited Company the annual accounts recorded sales of a £16,299. In general, the sales showed rising trend and in 1900-01 a value of £124,960 was recorded. The continually increasing success of his business made it possible for Sir Alfred, during 1897, to purchase and move his family to Breadsall Priory, a country estate a few miles north of Derby.

94

# 4B

# William Gilbert Haslam

William, born in 1855, was Alfred's younger brother. He served an apprenticeship at John Brown and Son Ltd in Sheffield then returned to Derby, during the 1880s, to work with Alfred as works manager and director.

He worked diligently and was the mainstay in helping Alfred to build up and manage the business, the production facilities and the staff. He would have been in charge of the factory when Alfred was away. Family descendants wrote that *he generated a strong feeling of personal loyalty among the workforce.*

*At a Workman's Banquet held in 1890, to celebrate Alfred becoming Mayor*, a guest Alderman Roe MP gave a toast "Success of the Haslam Foundry Engineering Co Ltd". He went on to say:-

> ... in addition, they had Mr. W.G Haslam - who was a good person anyone could find (Loud applause). His Worship could not always be present at his works, and he (Mr. Roe) did not know anyone in whom he could place more confidence than W.G. Haslam (Applause).

He married Susannah Mary Haigh on April 6, 1881, at Lindley near Huddersfield. They had three daughters and a son, Gerald Haigh who was employed at the factory. In 1921, Gilbert was named as a one of the directors of the Derby Pure Ice and Storage Company Ltd. This company was formed from the *'ice factory business'* that was part of the Haslam Company. When Sir Alfred died in 1927, William would have been 72 years of age. Nevertheless, he was named as a director in the companies that were subsequently formed and dissolved following sale of the Haslam Company. William's home was at 'North Lees', Duffield Road, this was Alfred's home before moving to Breadsall Priory

He was appointed a magistrate in 1916 and was a prominent freemason. He had a record of public service, being active in various local charitable institutions and hospitals. He was one of the founder members of Derby County Football Club; a former President of the Derbyshire Golf Club and a member Derbyshire Cricket Club Committee. Also, he was president of the Derbyshire Chess Club and the Derby Mechanics Institute. He was a prominent Baptist and a deacon of Osmaston Road Baptist Church, and ex–president of Derby Baptist Union and the Derby Free Church Council. For many years he was closely associated with The Derby Choral Union and became its President.

His funeral took place at Osmaston Road Baptist Church on April 1, 1935, the subsequent interment being at Uttoxeter Road Cemetery. William was just one month short of his 80th birthday. [*Derby Daily Telegraph* August 13 & March 28, 1935, plus *Derby Evening Telegraph* April 1, 1935]

# 5B

# Housing, Property and The Institute

As the profits of his Company increased, Alfred accumulated a portfolio of real estate for investment and rental income. An early example was building of houses in the Chester Green area. After 1876, the date of his Limited Company, Alfred needed to increase his workforce with skilled men to cope with the burgeoning work load.

He was the first to take advantage of the Council's decision to turn the footpath from City Road to Little Chester into a new street and sell land on either side for housing development. To attract and keep skilled men, in 1880, he purchased a piece of land on the North West corner and began to build 'cottages', both for the use of his workforce. These 'cottages' were small terraced houses with a cellar under the front room. To the rear were gardens and outhouses. Other builders quickly followed suit and single, paired and blocks of houses sprang up.

In 1885, Alfred bought the last available building plots on the east side of City Road and built a row of houses as far as the GNR embankment. The last house was given a third storey which punctuates the row, like a full stop. Oddly, there is no access to the upper space so perhaps this was simply an architectural nicety. Diamond patterns in the brick work are found here and on many of Alfred's houses.

He also built houses on Old Chester Road in the centre of the Roman area of occupation. Here, when foundations were dug in 1886, workmen found a quantity of Roman pottery and other artefacts. A cast iron plaque with the words 'Roman Camp' was made and set into the brickwork to record the site and for many years, people talked about living in the 'Camp Block'.

At the same time, Alfred invested in a more prestigious development on St. Paul's Road, newly pitched on the southern edge of The Green. He purchased the land for £1,775 2s. 6d. and raised it by 3 ft. to address the problem of flooding. Three terraced rows of 25 showpiece houses were built, four larger ones at each end for higher paid employees. Haslam employed three architects; passageways between each block of houses indicating the three phases. The first block of 13 houses was designed by Alexander MacPherson and built in 1884 while F. C. Coulthurst was the architect of 14-21. The final four houses, 21-25, were built to plans drawn up in 1891 by Derby architect James Wright, St James' Street.

The decorative tiling and timber work used in building these 'Arts and Crafts' style

St Paul's Road

houses reflect Alfred's new wealth. A typical dwelling had three downstairs rooms, the front for 'best', a living room at the rear off which a steep staircase ascended to three bedrooms, and a small kitchen. The larger houses had two attic rooms above. Heating was by open coal fires and the rooms were gas lit. In the kitchen, cold water was piped to a hand pump at the side of a stone sink and in one corner stood the wash day copper. Built-in cupboards and a walk-in pantry with a stone thrall provided storage space.

Running behind the houses was a lane for the night soil men who came round after dark with horse and cart to empty the cess pits. These were later replaced by an

Rostherne

outhouse toilet attached to the coal house. There was a yard for hanging out washing and enough space for a vegetable plot. The 1891 census gives an average of seven persons to a household; a youthful population with 67 children, almost one to every adult.

Alfred also built Seale Street facing St. Paul's Church, a terraced row designed by MacPherson in a more modest style. A covenant was placed on all these properties: *no foundry boilers, soap, candle, varnish, paint, white lead or glue manufacture `should be carried on there.* To the rear of the houses there were stables for Haslam's own use as he travelled by coach, almost daily, to the works from North Lees and later from Breadsall Priory.

Full details of Alfred's property portfolio are not known. As mentioned previously, he had purchased the 'Northlees and West Bank' estate on the west side of Duffield Road on which a plot had been used to build his home 'North Lees' in 1875. However, the remainder of this area, mostly open space, was not developed until after his death in 1927.

Then in 1890 he purchased a large acreage on the opposite side of the road. Here, he built several semi-detached villas. The first pair was designed by architects Naylor and Sale[24]. In 1895 four more villas were built, this time to the design of Coulthurst and Booty. These were named Rostherne, Kinross, Arundel and Killarney[25]. He also owned land on the nearby West Bank, Wheeldon Road and land to the rear of Parkfield House called Kedleston Field.

Another property that came on the market after his death, was advertised in the *Derby Daily Telegraph* on May 13 and June 10, 1927:-

One of the most important sales of property in Derby in recent years is announced for next Tuesday afternoon by auctioneers Richardson and Linnell. It holds an additional interest from it possibly being the ultimate selection of a site for the proposed new town hall and municipal buildings, the area being one of the two favoured by the special committee of the Corporation. The property, which is freehold, forms part the estate of the late Sir Alfred Haslam, and covers an area of 6,880 square yards. It comprises the shop and garage premises, numbers 30 to 34, London Road, Nos. 1 to 7, Victoria Buildings, with motor premises the rear, numbers 33 to 41, Osmaston Road, and a building site at The Spot. There is frontage to London Road of 317ft 4in. and to Osmaston Road of 168ft 8in. The situation close to the centre of the town makes it very valuable. Presently, the property produces an aggregate annual rental of £1,840. It will be first offered in one lot, and, if unsold, in separate lots.

## The Institute

Another property initiated by Alfred was the Institute, or Recreation Rooms, which stands at the corner of St Paul's Road and City Road. Designed by architect James Wright in 1895, it is an impressive building of 14 bays which curves round the corner and is ornamented with brick pilasters. Upstairs was an industrial space for two pattern rooms but on the ground floor an entrance hall led into a reading room, with a large mess room to the rear to cater for educational and recreational needs. It was often used for social events. The *Derby Mercury* reported a pre-Christmas tea and concert held there on December 9, 1896, soon after it was built:-

The institute has been built by Sir Alfred Haslam at considerable cost...... For a considerable time, the workers have wanted a place to hold social gatherings...... The building is a very spacious one...... In the daytime it is used as a mess room and in the evenings for literary/recreation...... it is managed by a committee of employees. Quite 300 sat down to a substantial tea and there were about twice that number at the subsequent concert...... Amongst those present, besides Sir Alfred and Lady Haslam were the Bishop of Derby plus other members of the Haslam family...... After tea the Bishop of Derby briefly addressed those present...... He hoped they would make the place as successful as possible... He hoped that the young men would go there at night so to be kept away from the curses of drink and gambling, which was the ruin of many (Hear hear)...... Sir Alfred was loudly applauded on rising. He said he had built the place for two purposes; one to be used as a mess room for the workmen and the other for their enjoyment... and to bring along their wives, sons and daughters (Applause)...... He was glad to see that short religious services were to be held once or twice a week. He had promised to supply a harmonium and he expected it to arrive next week (Applause)...... The concert programme was of a varied character and all the performers acquitted themselves admirably.

# 6B

# Serving the People of Derby: Mayor

As well as business interests Alfred spent much time on public affairs. In 1879 he stood for election to the Council as a representative of Derwent Ward. The *Derby Mercury* printed his election address on August 20, 1879:-

To the Electors of Derwent Ward, Ladies and Gentlemen

> By the retirement of your old representative, Mr James Parkins, a vacancy occurs in the Council. I am desired by a large number of Ratepayers to offer you my services. Having lived in the Borough nearly the whole of my life, and for many years carried on a large business in this Ward, I am well known to many of the electors. From the fact of being a large ratepayer and an employer of working men my interest in the affairs of the Town are in common with your own, and my efforts would be used in the direction of securing the most efficient management and a judicious expenditure of the public money.

> The continued increase of rates is a matter of great importance for all members of the community, and needs careful attention, or the manufacturing interests will be seriously crippled, and trade diverted from the Town.

> If it is your pleasure to elect me, it will be my earnest desire to further your Interests as far as possible. Your obedient servant Alfred Seale Haslam

He was elected and became very active in committee work of the Council. He became an Alderman in 1892 and remained in the Corporation until 1897 when he retired due to his move to live in Breadsall Priory, this being outside the Borough. From 1886 he was a Justice of the Peace for the Borough and in 1901 he became a County Magistrate. His local business interests were many; he was a Director of the Derby and Derbyshire Bank and for a number of years the Vice-President of the Chamber of Commerce. His social offices included the Presidency of the Derbyshire Children's Hospital and a Directorship of the Derbyshire Infirmary.

In 1890, he was unanimously elected to be Mayor of Derby for the year 1890 to 1891. As a celebration he arranged a banquet for his employees and their wives. This was held at the Drill Hall in Derby on December 20, 1890. The menu describes a lavish feast of eight courses, with about 750 people enjoying the occasion. The proceedings were accompanied by music, toasts, and speeches and the atmosphere was convivial. The *Derby Daily Telegraph* reporter recounted the scene in detail[19]:-

> The spacious hall was handsomely decorated with flags and evergreens, the orchestra in particular being in a perfect forest of plants and shrubs, and when the hour arrived for the commencement of the proceedings, the scene presented was in the highest degree animated and effective. Mr. Win. Crowther had charge of the music arrangements, which were most enjoyable, the glee singing being in several instances of a very high order. Dr. Corbett, the organist at All Saints' Church, presided at the organ, and during dinner played a selection of suitable airs, which were much enjoyed. In one or two instances the appropriateness of the music was promptly

recognised by the guests, who sang lustily such tunes as "Auld Lang Syne," etc. Mr. T. H. Wood during the evening sang "The Little Hero" which was heartily appreciated. We should not omit to mention that Mr. George Gilbert acted efficiently as toastmaster. It goes without saying that the task of catering for so formidable body of diners was not an easy one, especially on such bitter night as Saturday.

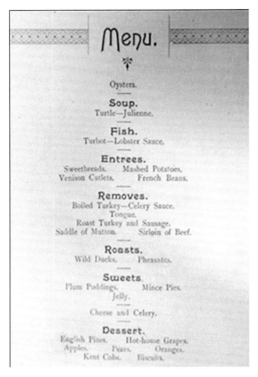

The food was provided by William Jerram of the County Hotel on St Mary's Gate:- In this connection it may be mentioned that the whole of the boiled meats and vegetables were cooked by gas at the Drill Hall, Messrs. Crump and Co. supplying a variety of appliances for this purpose, including a large hot closet for keeping the cooked meats warm preparatory to serving...

Personal friends, including members of the town council had been invited. When the mayoral party entered the Hall, around 5.30pm, they were received with *'loud and continuous cheering as they took their seats'*. At the end of the meal came a series of toasts starting with the 'Queen and Royal Family'. Mr Prince, the principal works foreman and a popular long-time member of the staff, then formally presented Alfred with an illuminated address, bound in crimson morocco, embellished with geometrical design and, and enclosed in a morocco, velvet lined cabinet. It was illuminated in the fifteenth century style:

> To A. Seale Esq.J.P. Dear Sir. - We, the employees of the Haslam Foundry and Engineering Co., Limited, Union Foundry, Derby, represented by the undersigned, do most heartily congratulate you on your elevation to the Mayoralty of this ancient Borough of Derby, and trust you will be given health and strength to carry out the arduous duties an important office entails...

Alfred, in reply, reminisced about the Company and their achievements and then, thanked Mr Prince for his long and faithful service and presented him with a marble timepiece with an inscription, *'Presented to Mr Henry Prince by the Mayor of Derby (A Seale Haslam, JP) to commemorate twenty three and a half years faithful service, Dec 20th 1890'*.

Alfred had membership of numerous local and national organisations. A few examples of these were: -

- President of the Institute of Refrigeration 1914-15
- President of the Derby Chamber of Commerce 1891 to 1894
- Member of The Executive Council of Associated Chambers of Commerce
- Director and Chairman of the Derby Canal Company
- President of the Derby Society of Engineers
- Member of the Institution of Mechanical Engineers

# Children's Fancy Dress Ball

In January 1891, when Alfred was Mayor of Derby it was announced that he and his wife would be hosting a Children's Fancy Dress Ball on February 3 at the Drill Hall Derby, this type of children's event being the first to be held in Derby.

THE MAYOR AND MAYORESS'S JUVENILE FANCY DRESS BALL

R. JEFFERSON & SONS,

ALBERT HOUSE, DERBY,

WILL HAVE ON VIEW FROM WEDNESDAY NEXT A SELECTION OF

BOYS' & GIRLS' FANCY COSTUMES,

FROM

SIMMONS'S, THE CELEBRATED COURT COSTUMIER,

8, KING-STREET, COVENT GARDEN, LONDON

COSTUMES FOR HIRE, OR MADE TO ORDER ON MODERATE TERMS.

JANUARY 19TH, 1891.          EARLY INSPECTION INVITED.

The evening was reported in detail by the *Derby Daily Telegraph*[21]. It proved to a popular event with 600 adults and 300 children present. The hall was 'radiant with light and colour'. Music was played throughout the evening by the Band from the Burton Volunteers which added to the great success of the event.

When guests started to arrive, *'huge crowds of sightseers thronged the approaches'*. The Mayor was accompanied by the Corporation's uniformed mace and standard bearers. A group of the Burton Volunteers lined the approach to the Hall plus two police sergeants dressed as beefeaters.

The Mayor and Mayoress received their guests in a handsomely fitted reception room as they passed by to the main hall. Alfred wore his Chain of Office and his wife Ann was attired in a dress of grey figured satin with a white chiffon, ornamented with ostrich feathers, she also carried a large bouquet of lilies of the valley. They were accompanied by:-

> Their four children, Victor, Hilda, Edith, and Eric, all of whom wore fancy costumes. Victor, the eldest son, attired the full uniform of a naval lieutenant, whilst his elder sister was prettily dressed the character Esmeralda, wearing skirt of crimson satin, beautifully embroidered with gold lace, and ornamented with sequins. Edith, his Worship's second daughter, represented a Swiss peasant girl, a somewhat simpler costume than her sister, but one equally as becoming. Eric, the youngest of the family, was attired the rich costume of court page the time of Charles the Second.

Prior to the main programme, guests promenaded around the hall while listening to music. After a couple of dances a procession was formed with the children, headed by Alfred's four children, marching several times four abreast around the room much to the delight and pleasure of the adults. The paper described the wide range of costumes:-

That we found familiar costumes representing the seasons of the year (particularly winter) was inevitable. Nor was the experience to be regretted, for the little ladies thus attired looked without exception most effective.

Equally as a matter of course, the heroes and heroines of the nursery were much in evidence. Many jovial little votaries of Terpsichore footed as Boy Blue, Little Miss Muffit, Old Mother Hubbard, Little Red Riding Hood, Mary, Mary quite contrary, Little Peep, and the rest of them.

Naturally, inspiration had been sought from the lyric and histrionic worlds. Opera was represented by such celebrities "Carmen","Bettina" ("La Mascotte"), "Figaro", "The Daughter of the Regiment", "Jack Point" and "Elsie Maynard" (The Yeoman of the Guard), "Katisha", (The Mikado), "The Toreador," and "Maritana," who were supported by the following among other dramatic notabilities: "David Garrick", "Little Lord Fauntleroy", "Tina" (My Sweetheart), "Mephstophiles", and the always welcome "Harlequin" and "Clown".

The patriotic services were to the fore, the Navy being especially well represented in every branch from Jack Tar to the Admiral himself. Our old Nobility found handsome representatives in Richard Duke of York and the Earl of Essex, whilst the interests of the legal profession were zealously watched by a Q.C. and townsmen in wigs and gowns.

With these illustrious beings were associated peasants and flower girls many climes, pages various periods, jesters, jockeys, and historical characters too numerous to mention.

A programme of children's and adult dances took place lasting until half past twelve then with the Mayor's permission the programme was extended by another hour. During the evening the photographer Mr Winter and his assistants- *by means of the new magnesium flash light, took two instantaneous photographs of the Hall and its gaily dressed inmates.*

Food was served under the supervision of Mr Kayner from the Bell Hotel. Due to the large number of guests it was - necessarily supplied in batches but their wants were well attended to. The supper menu was as follows:-

Salmon in mayonnaise, bear's head, gelatines of turkey aux perigord, roast turkeys and chickens, York hams, tongues, galantine chicken pistachios, spiced beef, pheasants, chicken in mayonnaise, lobster salads, Dantzic Victoria, Noyeau, and Macedoine jellies, Vanilla creams, French pastry assorted, trifles, ices, dessert, tea, coffee. Refreshments were supplied from a buffet at the lower end of the dancing-hall.

The entire evening went without a hitch and credit was given to the staff who efficiently managed the event. A complete list of guests and children plus their costumes was included in the newspaper report.

In the same paper there was a letter from a Mr A Hamilton, proposing parents co-operate in presenting the Mayoress with an album containing photographs of their children in fancy dress as a memento of the occasion.

This proposal was taken up resulting, seven months later, in presentation of an album, to the Mayoress (now Lady Haslam). It was made on Saturday afternoon September 19, 1891, at the home of the Mayor on Duffield Road, Derby. The organisers, Mr. A. B. Hamilton, Mr. Hobson, and Mr Sowter, were present and the gift was informally presented with a few words by Mr Hamilton to Lady Haslam who was accompanied by Sir Alfred and three of their children. The newspaper article recorded:-

> This souvenir took the form of six elegantly bound volumes, the size of a quarto portrait album, and each containing 24 portraits. The photographs had been executed in the beautiful platinotype form, delicately tinted paper, and were mounted by a patent process. The volumes were bound in dark maroon morocco, ornamented with gilt lettering and borders, and presented a most attractive appearance. The title page was the work of Mr. George Bailey, of Crompton Street, and is therefore a real work of art. It contains the Mayor's armorial bearings, well as the Borough Arms, and the following inscription: —"Presented by her guests to the Mayoress of Derby (Mrs. Alfred Scale Haslam), souvenir of the happy evening spent at the Children's Fancy Dress Ball, given by the Mayor and Mayoress on the 3rd February, 1891."

> The first portrait in the volumes was appropriately that 'Our Host' (the Mayor), then comes that of 'Our Hostess' (the Mayoress), which are followed by those of the members of their family, viz., Mr. Alfred Victor Haslam, Miss Hilda Anne, Miss Edith Hannah Haslam, and Master Eric Seale Haslam, in fancy dress.

Sir Alfred, on behalf Lady Haslam, cordially returned thanks for the gift, which he said he and his wife would ever highly value, and that it would be landed heirloom to their family [*Derby Daily Telegraph* September 24, 1891].

# Knighthood: Arise Sir Alfred

The highlight of Alfred's year (1890-1891) as Mayor was the visit to Derby of Queen Victoria and the laying of the foundation stone of the Derbyshire Royal Infirmary.

Profits from his fifteen-year-old company had increased steadily and by this time he was a very wealthy man. This portrait [National Portrait Gallery], by Alexander Bassano, taken during the 1890s perhaps shows him at the pinnacle of his achievements, still sharp and active but his hair and beard now white.

**Sir Alfred Seale Haslam**
(*National Portrait Gallery*)

An overriding issue, in Derby, at that time was the dire need for a new hospital. The Derbyshire General Infirmary had been built in 1810, with an underfloor hot-air heating system devised by William Strutt which was an innovation at the time. By 1890 the warren of flues which distributed the heat around the building was not only carrying heat but also a myriad of infections, compounded by a leakage of effluent from the drainage system. Patients and nursing staff were beginning to die and temporary huts had been set up in the grounds while a solution was found.

In 1890 the Hospital Board, chaired by Sir William Evans, appointed a Building Committee to decide the best course of action. On June 29, 1890, that Committee recommended demolition and London architects Young and Hall were commissioned to design the replacement building[22]. At this time, before the introduction of income tax, all the funds had to be raised locally and an appeal was launched.

Alfred, with his customary zeal and initiative, wrote to Queen Victoria to ask her to come to Derby to lay the foundation stone. A prompt reply was forthcoming with the date of May 21, 1891. On that date, a dull, chilly Thursday, the Queen broke her annual train journey to Scotland at Derby railway station to make a State visit and lay the first stone in a temporary building hastily improvised at short notice on the site.

Alfred had made lavish preparations for the visit, bearing the cost himself. The reception party greeted the Queen and her entourage at a magnificent floral and evergreen arch at the station entrance and escorted her carriage along the Midland Road, festooned with pink and white roses. A series of Venetian poles linked together with evergreens lined London Road as the procession made its way into the centre of Derby so that, 'the whole of the progress of Her Majesty lay through bowers of flowers and evergreens, the waving of thousands of flags adding brightness and joyousness to her path'[23]. At the entrance to St James' Street a floral canopy had been erected and the Market Place, at the centre of proceedings, was decked out with floral swags and flags.

The High Sheriff, county gentry, clergy and the other dignitaries who formed the reception party were conveyed in twelve carriages. Amongst this grand elite procession, in the last two carriages were the four eldest Haslam children. Alfred Victor and Edith travelled in the eleventh carriage and Eric, wearing a 'Scottish costume' and Hilda occupied the twelfth and final carriage with Alfred and their mother.

**Queen Victoria laying foundation stone for the New Infirmary.**
**Alfred and his wife are on her left side**

When the Queen eventually arrived, late in the afternoon, she was greeted with music and Alfred presented an illuminated Address in a casket. Several more Addresses followed before the party moved off to the laying of the Foundation Stone.

At the end of the day on their return to the railway station, in the presence of his wife and children, Alfred was asked whether he would accept a knighthood. Having signified his pleasure, he was ushered into a room on the station platform which had been set aside and decorated in *regal splendour* for the Queen's use:-

> Here the Queen with the sword of the Lord Chamberlain, bestowed the accolade on the Mayor, who rose as "Sir Alfred". The Queen also several times and in the heartiest possible manner thanked the Mayor as representing the town for the excellence of the arrangements, the beauty of the decorations and above all – for this had touched her Majesty most dearly - the enthusiastic loyalty which "her people of Derby" had accorded her. The Queen who three times in the course of the interview gave Lady Haslam her hand to kiss, then took her farewell of the Mayor and the Mayoress and shortly afterwards departed for Carlisle, en route to Scotland.

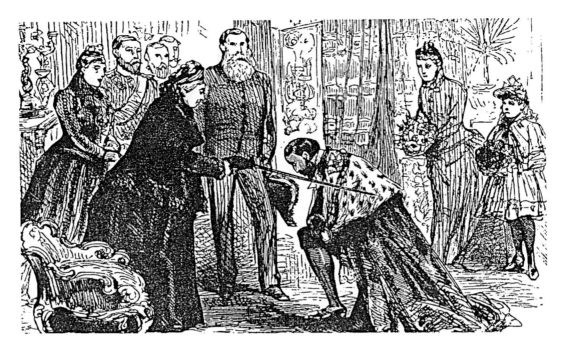

During the proceedings, Sir Alfred famously presented the Queen with a basket of apples shipped on a vessel fitted with a Haslam refrigeration system. These were from a cargo of 24,000 cases that had arrived from Tasmania only a few days previously. The bestowing of the Knighthood appeared to be spontaneous. However, Victorians were 'sticklers' for protocol and the opinion 'passed down' by relatives was that it must have been prearranged.

After the Royal party had left to continue their journey to Scotland, a Grand Mayoral Banquet was held, again at Alfred's expense, in a Marque erected at the Midland Hotel lit by the newly arrived electricity. The chef had been given carte blanche and the food was exceptional and there were fine wines for every course. Toasts and speeches followed: Alfred's brothers were present and the Rev. John Haslam responded to a toast on behalf of the Ministers of the Free Churches. What was most notable about his speech is the praise he bestowed on their late father:-

> Nothing during his life had affected him so much as the references made by all the speakers to his honoured father, when the Mayor was installed. It showed how good men influenced society after they were dead, and he was sure his brother would also say that he owed his character and his success largely to the sacrifices of an honoured father, who lived for his children, and whose memory is blessed.

The triumph was capped by a letter confirming Alfred's request that the word Royal be added to the name of the new hospital: hence the Derbyshire Royal Infirmary.

After the events were over, Alfred took personal responsibility for the publishing a 'Permanent Record of the Queen's Visit'[23]. The task of collecting and editing the material was given to W. Hobson at the *Derbyshire Advertiser* and a book in a navy card cover, lettered in gold, appeared within the year. In addition to an illustrated description of the Queen's visit and a brief description of the new Infirmary, biographies of Sir William Evans and Alfred were included.

# 9B

# St Paul's Church, Chester Green

During a tea and concert event held for his workers at the Institute in 1896 Sir Alfred concluded his speech by saying:-

> With the permission of the worthiest Bishop he had decided to erect the south aisle to the St Paul's Church (loud applause) and he hoped the work would be commenced in the near future. The people in that district and the town generally would then have something in commemoration of the Queen's long *reign* (Applause).

The new aisle was to commemorate the Diamond Jubilee (60 years) of the reign of Queen Victoria. Ceremonial laying of the foundation stone for the aisle took place on Saturday, May 8, 1897. It was preceded by a short service in the church conducted by the Bishop of Derby and other clergy. Lord and Lady Haslam were amongst those present.

Afterwards a procession was formed to the site of the new aisle. Lady Haslam laid the stone, after it had been consecrated by the Bishop, with a silver trowel presented to her for the purpose by the church council. A hearty vote of thanks was given to Lady Haslam and Sir Alfred returned the thanks. The proceedings were terminated by singing of the National Anthem. [*Derby Mercury* May 12, 1897]

Erection of the aisle was completed by December 1897. A service of dedication was held on December 4, 1897, the Lord Bishop of Southwell leading the service. Sir Alfred and Lady Haslam were in the congregation. The aisle had been built, at a cost of £800, using Coxbench stone to match the church, providing additional seating for 100 people. Other improvements had been made, the principal ones being moving the pulpit from the right to the left of the Chancel for the convenience of the new aisle and the choir vestry from the end of the church to the south transept, [*Derby Mercury* December 8, 1897]. Previously, during 1895, Sir Alfred had replaced the church's organ.

# 10B

# The Move to Breadsall Priory 1897

**East Front Breadsall Priory    Photo by A Victor Haslam**
*Derby Archaeological Society*

In 1897, Alfred bought Breadsall Priory 4½ miles north of Derby. This was a large house in a rural setting which had been built in the sixteenth century on the site of a small Augustinian priory and subsequently much added to. It had a long and sometimes distinguished list of owners, most notably Erasmus Darwin. Richard Rainshaw Rothwell, from whom Alfred purchased it had owned it for seven years.

Rothwell put the house and estate into auction in July 1897 but Alfred bought it in August by private treaty. The auction catalogue described it as 'a very picturesque and interesting stone-built castellated Mansion House', occupying 'an enviable position in a delightful and unusually well-timbered park with an undulating character and is surrounded by perfectly matured pleasure gardens' which included a flower garden fish ponds and a romantic wilderness walk, through which flowed a stream. More practically, it also came with good stabling, a kitchen garden and a home farm attached to 135 acres of land, mainly grassland. Rothwell had provided the house with ample water by creating a reservoir which could hold 30,000 gallons, and he had installed electricity throughout.

In keeping with ownership of a country house, the household was increased with the addition of a Butler, Arthur Alfred Turvey in addition to a Cook, Annie Robinson, a maid, Mary French, two housemaids, Kate Greatorex and Elizabeth Thorley, and governess Brydon Jones. The purchase was made just too late for celebrations of Alfred Victor's 21st birthday, which were held at Matlock.

Alfred set about extending and further modernising the Priory. His house North Lees had been stripped of its oak panelling and this was fitted into the dining room, covering the lower part of the walls while leaving the upper walls free for picture hanging. An over mantel from North Lees was placed above the fireplace. The mantlepiece being a carved representation in oak of in 'mine host receiving his guests in'.

Outside the dining room, at the foot of the main stairs, Alfred installed the large Gothic style door made by his father for display at the Great Exhibition in 1851 as an example of ancient church wrought iron-work. The drawing room was accessed from the entrance hall by a separate flight of stairs running parallel to the main staircase.

A library was created in the existing billiard room and a large new wing added at the west end of the south front, with a new oak panelled billiard room complete with minstrel gallery and decorated in Moorish style. At the west end of the south front Haslam built a gable matching Morley's replica gable of 1861. Haslam's coat of arms and the date 1899 were placed above the library's bay window. In a room on the ground floor below the billiard room was a small windowless area for use as a photographic dark room. This was used by Haslam's eldest son, Alfred Victor Haslam, a keen photographer.

Alfred was immensely proud of his new house and commissioned *An Illustrated History of Breadsall Priory* which was published in 1900. This he sent to family members, friends and even slight acquaintances. Sometimes the 'History' was sent with an invitation to come and view, as instanced by a reply from Sir Alfred Hickman of Wightwick Hall, a Midlands industrialist and steel magnate.

> My dear Sir Alfred, Best thanks for the most interesting history & description of Breadsall Priory. It must be a charming place. I must also thank you for your kind invitation of which I hope someday to avail myself. My wife joins with me in kindest regards and best wishes. Yours sincerely Alfred Hickman

In 1911 he had several hundred postcards of the house reproduced to send to friends and acquaintances. Two views were chosen from the many photographs taken by Alfred Victor before his death in 1907, and these were sent for reproduction to Charles Barrow Keene (1863-1937), a Derby photographer with premises on Iron Gate. Apparently, the negatives were unfortunately misplaced as shown by this letter:-

November 27, 1911

> Dear Sir, As promised when I saw you the other day, I have been up to Mrs Victor Haslam's and been through all the films she has. I have also set a different assistant to entirely empty our store negative cupboard and go through each packet under every name to check any chance of error in the wrappers but it is all still without success. Undoubtedly the negatives were returned to Mr Victor when printed. I am sorry I cannot find them and so set the matter at rest. Yours respectfully, C. B. Keene

Due to this interest in Archaeology, in 1904, he invited two Archaeology members, local architect Percy H. Currey, and Reverend Charles Cox to explore Breadsall Priory. In the cellar they found evidence of the original Priory. Their findings were written up in 1905 in two articles published in the Society Journal which include photographs by Alfred Victor and sketches by Currey[27].

Alfred applied for a Coat of Arms from the College of Arms and this was granted. The Grant in the 9th edition of Fox-Davies *Armorial Families reads*:-

Knight Bachelor. Justice of the Peace for the county of Derby, Born Oct. 27, 1844 being the fourth son of William Haslam of Derby, his wife Ann, daughter of Joseph Smith of Branstone, Staffordshire; dubbed Knight Bachelor 1891. Clubs: Devonshire, City of London, Reform. Livery: Blue coat with white collar and cuffs and silver buttons. He bears for **Arms**: Argent, two bars wavy azures on a chief engrailed gules a lamb statant, between two hazel leaves proper. Upon the escutcheon is placed a helmet befitting his degree, with a mantling azure and argent. For his **Crest,** upon a wreath of the colours, an eagle rising regardant, holding in the beak a hazel-leaf slipped proper, and pendent from the neck by a riband argent an escutcheon gules, charged with a Iamb statant proper; with the **Motto** "Agnus Dei salvator meus" (*Lamb of God's Salvation*).Estates: Breadsall Priory and Little Chester in the County of Derby. Seat: Breadsall Priory.

The Arms were carved in stone and set into the south gable of the new wing he was building at Breadsall Priory. Apparently, the lamb on the shield and 'lamb' included in the motto symbolically represents the 'meat trade'. Also, an image of a lamb on the pendant around the neck of the eagle represents transport of the meat.

# 11B

# Alfred's Sons, Coming of Age

In 1897 there was much to celebrate when Alfred's eldest son Alfred Victor's 21st birthday. He was born on June 24, 1876, and attended Repton School, Derbyshire from January 1891 to July 1893[3].

At 18 years of age he had joined his father's staff and trained as an engineer and became a Member of The Institution of Mechanical Engineers. He eventually became one of the principals of the business and was co-works manager alongside W G Haslam. For some time, he was a Captain in the K Company of the Derby Volunteers until, due to 'business pressure', he resigned his commission. He was a keen photographer and at one time was Secretary of the Derby Photographic Society. Examples of his work are in the Record Office at the British Museum.

**Alfred Victor Haslam**

In June 1897, employees of the Company marked his 21st birthday with a presentation to him in the Works Institute. The gift comprised a dressing case, travelling bag, and walking stick. As well as marking his 'coming of age' the gift was in appreciation of the interest he had taken in the welfare of the employees together with his assistance in the formation of the Institute management. Family celebrations were also held to mark Victor's birthday. Sir Alfred did not fail to include the workforce in the festivities. In September 1897 *St. Paul's Parish Magazine* reported:-

> To celebrate this happy event, Sir Alfred and Lady Haslam invited the workmen of the Haslam Works and their wives and the tenants, together numbering between 800 and 900, to a Garden Party in the Pavilion grounds, Matlock on Saturday, August 29.

They were conveyed by two special trains and spent a very enjoyable afternoon in visiting the principal sights in Matlock, for which they were provided with free tickets. At five o'clock they sat down to a substantial tea in the Pavilion:-

---

**Derbyshire Advertiser** May 8, 1903

During a thunderstorm which broke over Derby on Tuesday afternoon Sir Alfred Haslam and his son Mr Victor Haslam, had a narrow escape of being seriously injured. They were about to proceed home to Breadsall Priory in a pony carriage, and had just driven through the wide entrance gates into the street, when there was a very heavy clap of thunder. This frightened the pony which became restive and beyond the control of the driver. It plunged into one of iron supports of the railings round Chester Green, and the shafts of the carriage snapping, the pony got away. The carriage remained where it was and the occupants were able to retain their seats. It was a narrow escape. Sir Alfred and his son afterwards proceeded home in a cab.

---

... A sight not soon forgotten it was to see that immense building packed with men and women brim-full with jollity and good humour, joining heartily in the rejoicing of their esteemed employer and his Lady.

A photograph was taken and sports followed which included a tug of war, a trial of strength very popular with the work force. The fitting shop fielded three teams to challenge the pattern shop, the foundry workers and the smiths.

Seven years later Victor married Ethel Woodiwiss on July 5, 1904, at St John's Church, Hazlewood. The bride's father was Alderman Woodiwiss who had been twice Mayor of Derby. The reception was at the family home in Duffield where about 300 guests attended. (*Belper News* July 8, 1904)

After the couple returned from honeymoon in North Devon, Alfred and Lady Haslam invited all the Company's staff and employees together with their wives them during a gathering at Breadsall Priory. It was a fine day and the guests, numbering about 700, were conveyed to Breadsall by special trains, although some preferred to walk.

**Company Workforce and Wives at Breadsall Priory to meet newly married Victor Haslam and his wife, 1904** *Haslam Papers*

They were entertained by the band of the Volunteer Battalion. The whole party including the Haslam family gathered together for a photograph. Sir Alfred and Victor gave speeches. After the photograph had been taken the party was then free to inspect the grounds, be entertained by a Punch and Judy show or indulge in an 'Aunt Sally' and other games. Luncheon was served in two sittings in a marquee on a nearby field. A vote of thanks was given by a staff member to end the day. [*Derbyshire Advertiser* August 26, 1904]

Victor and Ethel had a son, Victor Ronald Seale (1905-1950), born on 12 July and baptised at All Saints, Derby on July 14, 1905. Two years later, tragically, Victor (Senior) suffered an illness which lasted several months (probably pleurisy) and died on the night of February 27, 1907, aged 30 years. The funeral and burial were at Morley church on March 5 attended by his parents, family, friends and representatives from the works. He is commemorated by a window in the Church[28]. The death of Victor, being the eldest son, must have been a tragic shock to the Haslam family. Because he was a principal of the company, he most likely would have succeeded his father in running the business.

Eric, the second son, joined the firm. Born in 1886, he attended Haileybury School Hertfordshire from 1900 to 1904. His 21st birthday was on April 8, 1907, and by then he was working at the Company. To celebrate his coming of age workmen made a presentation to him. Due to the death of his brother Victor in March the ceremony was postponed until May and 'would be of a very quiet character'. The present comprised 'a handsome dressing and travelling bag, silver mounted and containing a set of cut-glass bottles and jars, with silver tops. The event was held in the Institute. Eric thanked the men saying he highly appreciated their good wishes and feelings.

**Eric Haslam**

On his 21st birthday, the Staff presented Eric with an elaborately oak carved wall aneroid barometer, with supporting griffins, and surmounted by an 8-day clock, made by James Hicks of London and inscribed on a silver plate: *Presented to Eric Seale Haslam by the Staff of The Haslam Foundry & Engineering Co Ltd upon his coming of age on April 8 1907*. An address accompanying the gift wished Eric long life and health in assisting with work of the Company. There was no formal presentation; the gift was sent to Breadsall Priory[29].

William Kenneth, the third son, was born on March 10, 1893, and attended Repton School, Derbyshire from 1907 to 1911[3]. He started at Trinity College, Cambridge in June 1911[10] as a fee-paying student but did not graduate[10] and joined the Haslam Company.

Upon his 21st birthday, March 10, 1914, he was presented by members of the Works staff with *a beautifully engraved gold match box, suitab*ly inscribed. In June, Sir Alfred invited office staff and foremen to a garden party at Breadsall Manor. The weather was lovely and tennis and lawn games were played. Musical entertainment was provided the band of the Derbyshire Imperial Yeomanry.

**William Kenneth Haslam**

Tea was provided on the lawn and family members made sure it was an enjoyable occasion[38]. During the Great War (1914-1918) Kenneth joined the Royal Field Artillery and gained the rank of Captain.

# 12B

# Queen Victoria's Statues

**Queen Victoria Statue
Newcastle-under-Lyme**

Being now – 'Sir Alfred' - he decided to present statues of Queen Victoria to places with which he had established a strong connection. The statues were taken from a marble original sculpted by C B Birch and were cast in bronze. They were 9 ft high and mounted on a granite pedestal of similar height and 6ft 4in square.

The first statue was presented to the London Corporation and erected at the north end of Blackfriars Road Bridge. It was unveiled on July 21, 1896, and still stands in the middle of the busy road.

From 1901 to 1903, Sir Alfred was the Mayor of Newcastle under Lyme. He presented the second statue to the Borough to commemorate the 1902 Coronation of Edward VII. The Grand Duke Michael of Russia (Lord High Steward of the Borough of Newcastle under Lyme) unveiled the statue on November 5, 1903. After the ceremony, 450 guests sat down to a luncheon. During a speech, after the meal, Sir Alfred mentioned that he was prepared to present a similar statue to Derby. Explaining why, he said that, during 1891, while Mayor of Derby there was difficulty in raising funds for a new hospital. However, when it became known that Queen Victoria had consented to lay the foundation stone:

> Funds at once jumped from £12,000 to £40,000; Derby having now a fine hospital and nurses on which £12,000 had been expended. *For* this reason, he wished to honour the memory of Queen Victoria[33].

A third statue was given to the town of Derby and erected on 'The Spot' in Derby in 1906. During this year the Royal Agricultural Society show was held on Osmaston Park. Derby.  King Edward VII visited Derby on June 28 to visit the show. He travelled by train and alighted at Nottingham Road Station. After a welcoming ceremony at the Guildhall the Royal cortege approached 'The Spot':-

Sir Alfred and his party arrived first, then the Mayor, and then the royal carriage. Holding the string which would unveil the statue Alfred approached the carriage and invited the King to perform the ceremony. Owing to the rain the string would not move easily and the King experienced great difficulty. Sir Alfred looked unutterable things until a sailor came to the front, climbed the statue and loosened the slip knot to a round of applause. The King gave a reply and thanked Sir Alfred for his kindness before travelling on to the Show. [*Derby Daily Telegraph*, June 28, 1906, and January 15, 1927]

**Unveiling Queen Victoria Statue 1906 Derby**
*WW Winter Ltd*

During 1928, due to road traffic improvements, the statue was removed to the grounds of the Derbyshire Royal Infirmary, the foundation stone for this having been laid by Queen Victoria in 1891.

# Newcastle-under-Lyme and Parliament

After his Mayoral year Alfred was made an Alderman of Derby and turned his thoughts towards a seat in Parliament. He contested Derby as a Liberal Unionist in 1892 alongside William Hextall. Their Conservative opponents were Sir William Harcourt and Sir Thomas Roe. It was a lively contest and drew forth a set of doggerel verses from one of the Liberal Unionist supporters, printed in *The Derby Ram* on June 24, 1892. In spite of the poetic appeal Hextall and Haslam lost the contest.

In 1895, he stood for Derby once again but the Conservative party won. The two members returned were Sir Henry Howe Bemrose and Geoffrey Drage.

It was not until after the move to Breadsall that he looked elsewhere and found in the town of Newcastle-under-Lyme in Staffordshire a possible seat. His connections to Newcastle, initially, were not strong and he was not a regular member of the Council. However, he was approached to serve as Mayor, which he did for three consecutive years from 1901 to 1903 and stand for election in the 1900 election. He accepted the offer and was elected as a Liberal Unionist.

He was greeted by Benjamin Stone with his camera when he arrived at Parliament to take his seat. Photographs, taken outside the Speakers' Gate in March 1901, show him as a typical City gentleman, immaculately turned out in frock coat and top hat. Although only 57 years old, his hair is snow white and he has the appearance of a man of greater age[30]. He served as MP for the borough from October 1, 1901, to January 12, 1906, but was defeated in that year's election by Colonel Josiah Wedgwood.

---

**THE ASPIRATES ASPIRATIONS**

Harcourt, Haslam, Hextall, Roe,
Alphabetically so,

On the ballot paper go –

How they'll finish time must show.

Aspirates no less than three, Pride of place for William V., Alfred next, then William B, Lastly Tommy R-O-E.

Harcourt primus and Roe the worst! So they may be seen at first;

But when Harcourt's bubble's burst, aspirates will be reversed.

Ye Hextallites and Haslamites

Stand up for Old England's rights,

See how your gallant charge affrights

The Harcourtites and Dittoites

Fling no mud, the foolish plan Which vulgar Labby here began, But show the world how Derby can Appreciate her "Dead meat Man".

*Sir Alfred Haslam
M.P. for Newcastle-under-Lyme. 1901.*

**National Portrait Gallery**

He took the new role of an MP seriously. Although a very able speaker he made only one speech on February 10, 1904, while sitting in Westminster. This was, albeit a lengthy one, on a motion in the King's speech, on the subject of free trade and the difficulties of keeping a workforce in employment. He was concerned by the increasing indebtedness of the nation and although he would in the past have supported and a believer in free trade, the economic situation was very different now to that of the 1860s and he feared for the future if some action was not taken[31].

After his term as an MP, in 1905 Alfred was given the Freedom of the Borough of Newcastle. James Horlick (1844-1921) sent his congratulations.

November 13, 1905, Cowley Manor

> My dear Sir Alfred, my hearty Congratulations upon the honour conferred upon you in being presented with the freedom of Newcastle-under-Lyme. How very gratifying it must be to you & yours to know that the valuable work you have done for the borough is so much appreciated.

James Horlicks was a pharmacist and the co-founder with his brother William, of the firm of malted milk drinks. The firm was set up in Wisconsin in 1873 and later, in 1906, a factory was built in England, in Slough.

Alfred stood again in January 1906 but was defeated by a surge of support for the Conservative party. Rupert A Llewellyn Esq, honorary secretary to the Newcastle-under-Lyme Joint Unionist Association, wrote a polite letter, dated May 23, 1906:-

> Dear Sir Alfred - A numerously attended meeting of the Executive Council was held the Conservative Club Wolstanton on the 24th April and it was proposed by J Newton seconded by G K Downing and supported by Mr C H Bowers and unanimously passed:- 'That the very best thanks of this Executive Council be tendered to Sir Alfred Seale Haslam for the able and strenuous manner in which he contested the seat for the Parliamentary Borough of Newcastle-under-Lyme in the interest of the Unionist Cause at the General Election in January last.' I have much pleasure in conveying this resolution to you and trust that you are feeling much better for the holiday which you have been able to take. I remain, Dear Sir Alfred, Yours faithfully

After the election a group of defeated MPs including Alfred formed the 1900 Club. He was a member until he resigned in 1919. There is a letter from T. Conryn Platt, the Club Secretary, 4, Pickering Place (three doors below Lock, the hatter), St. James' Street, which gives a reason:-

April 9, 1919

> Dear Sir Alfred I quite understand, though the idea of an original member leaving the Club, strikes me sadly. But there it is. I know the Committee will be equally sad. Need I say how much I sympathise with you in your terrible bereavement: it all seems so dreadfully sad, and so young too. But you have indeed done your duty well in this terrible war in that you have given a hero to the Country.

The bereavement mentioned referred to the death of his son Kenneth William who was killed during 1917 in the Great War.

# 14B

# Visit to India 1902: Kedleston

In November 1902, the *Belfast News* reported that Alfred was sailing to India to attend the Coronation Durbar in Delhi as one of the guests of Viceroy George Curzon, the son of Nathaniel, Fourth Baron Scarsdale[32].

> **George Nathaniel Curzon- Marquess Curzon of Kedleston** (1859-1925) was a politician, Secretary of State for Foreign Affairs, and Viceroy of India. He entered Parliament as an MP in 1886. He spent much of the next eight years travelling around the world. He served in various government roles before being appointed Viceroy of India in 1899.

The Durbar, which lasted for about 10 days, took place in a tented city created on a vacant area of land. It was arranged by the Viceroy to celebrate the Accession of Edward VII and Queen Alexandria as Emperor and Empress of India, the Duke of Connaught acting as the King's representative.

**Lord and Lady Curzon on Elephant**
*Bourne & Shepherd's Photo Biographic- 'Coronation Durbar 1903.'*

It began on December 29, 1902, with a parade of elephants, the main event being on New Year's Day 1903. All the maharajahs and their retinues were in attendance - *perhaps the greatest collection of jewel as seen in one place.*

During his time in India Alfred attended a dinner at Government house in Calcutta[9]. *The Homeward Mail from India, China and the Far East'* (April 4, 1903) reported that he had returned to England after a prolonged tour of India, Burma and Ceylon.

Alfred appeared to have become acquainted with, Baron Scarsdale, because six letters exist written by hand on headed notepaper from his stately home Kedleston Hall, situated a few miles north of Derby.

July 25, 1909

> Dear Sir A Haslam, I shall hope to come over very shortly, & will write the day before. I will see the Spectator. Yours truly Scarsdale.

March 18, 1914

> Dear Sir Alfred Haslam, My great Hall & Saloon are a maze of scaffolding due to repairs & decoration & entirely closed but you are welcome to see several of the principal rooms still available and the church which has been beautifully restored by Lord Curzon – tomorrow would be a convenient day if it suits you. I remain yrs very truly    Scarsdale

Baron Scarsdale died on March 23, 1916. The following letters are written by his son Francis Nathaniel Curzon (1865-1941).

March 25, 1916

> Dear Sir Alfred - It will be very kind of you to come. Lunch here 1.30 pm. Yours. Curzon

Probably this is in reply to a card announcing the funeral on March 28, 1916.

April 2 (undated but by context 1916)

> Dear Sir Alfred May I in the name of my family thank you very sincerely not only for attending my father's funeral on such an inclement day, but also for your extremely kind thought in sending such a beautiful wreath - We have placed it over his coffin which lies in the vault. Believe me, Yours very truly, Francis N Curzon

Relatively few people attended the funeral which was held at Kedleston - 'only a small attendance of friends'...... 'and of members of the general public' as a snowstorm had swept over the district earlier in the day and only 'had abated but slightly'. The Derby Daily Telegraph reported that the service took place in the Marble Hall while a snowstorm raged outside, and a large body of mourners then proceeded to the church, though numbers were reduced.

# 15B

# Adventures in Germany: Hilda's Engagement

In the 1900s Alfred began to suffer from ill health and failing eye sight and from 1906 he was making annual trips to Germany to take the cure at Bad Homburg, a fashionable German spa town. His daughters Hilda and Edith would accompany him and in 1910 they extended their journey to the village of Oberammergau in Bavaria to watch the Passion Play, first performed in 1634, which takes place only every ten years.

**Hilda Haslam**

On their visit to Bad Homburg in 1912 they dined with Edward Carson KC, (a celebrated lawyer who had made his name as the prosecutor in the trial of Oscar Wilde in 1895). Carson was Irish and a leading Irish Ulster Unionist which accorded with Sir Alfred's political views. He was also prominent in the 1900 Club, of which Haslam was a founder member. On their return home, both Sir Alfred and Edith wrote to him with an invitation to stay at Breadsall.

This was a busy time for Carson and he politely refused, writing in his own hand. Later replies became increasingly abrupt, perhaps as he became fully immersed in Irish affairs.

Hilda's engagement to Rev. Herbert Ham was announced in the press on June 23, 1914[20]. In July Alfred, his daughters and a small group of friends met once again at St. Pancras station to make the journey to Bad Homburg and to stay as usual at the Victoria Hotel. Amongst the party was Baron James Joicey (1846-1936) plus members of his family and staff.

**Edith with elder sister Hilda**

Joicey was a Durham colliery magnate, like Sir Alfred a self-made millionaire and a Liberal Unionist Member of Parliament in 1901-5. James Joicey & Co in 1907 employed 12,000 people. After his peerage in 1905, he bought Ford Castle in Northumberland, a house and estate at Chester le Street which is now a residential activities centre. The following year, 1908, he bought the adjoining Etal estate.

The party left London by train on July 28 in good spirits. Why Sir Alfred and his friends chose this date to travel is not clear, particularly as they must have known of the general unrest and political interchanges happening in Europe since the assassination of Austrian Archduke Francis Ferdinand a month earlier, on June 28 at Sarajevo by a member of a Serbian terrorist gang. This act led to a declaration of war by Austria-Hungary, an act supported by the German government, on the very day of their departure.

Alfred later gave a report of his experiences to the *Derby Daily Telegraph*[37]. He said that after crossing the German border he noticed, while passing through Cologne, how quiet the station was and that the river bridge was guarded. In Bad Homburg they received news of fighting in Serbia, and of the German mobilisation against Russia and decided to return home but the German government had taken control of the railways for troop movements. Sir Alfred and Joicey managed to send a message home via Sweden but subsequently no communication was possible. There was nothing to do but wait in the hotel along with travellers of various nationalities.

In the days which shortly followed, Russia, an ally of Serbia, began mobilisation to help the Serbs. An alliance existed between Russia and France. The 'domino' effect was that Germany declared war on Russia on August 1 and then France on August 3. To invade France, Germany would have to violate Belgium's neutrality causing Britain reluctantly to declare war on Germany on August 4.

English subjects were told that they might be able to leave on August 5 but sentries were posted and they became prisoners of war and told not to leave the hotel. Eventually, after the false promises of a train, a group of 17 people including Sir Alfred and daughters and Lord Joicey were allowed to board a train to Cologne at one in the morning on Sunday 9 having been provided with passes from the American Embassy. Lord Joicey had to leave behind a son, probably his youngest named Drever, who was perhaps unwell, his daughter Marguerite, her maid Kate Farley and Doctor Barty King.

It was a slow journey on a winding route, but all went well at first as they travelled through Frankfurt and Cologne which they reached on Sunday evening. They then travelled to Goch, a town near the frontier, where they had to stay overnight. Next day they travelled to Wesel to see the Area Commander where they were put under armed guard and cross-examined. Here no British men between the age of 17 and 58 were allowed to cross the frontier as they were judged to be of military age; half a dozen of the group had to stay behind. These included Joicey's 'valets' and a schoolmaster, Charles Leveson Gower, a relation of the Duke of Sutherland.

Eventually the rest received a group 'passport' to continue but at the frontier there was another setback when the guards had to be convinced to accept the document. Finally, they crossed to safety in Holland (probably August 12). They sailed from Flushing to London on August 19 and there separated.

The Haslam party arrived '*safe and well but much tired* at Breadsall Priory in the early hours of the next morning. The ordeal caused Sir Alfred much anxiety and he was confined to bed for a few days suffering from severe shock to his nerves. They had been forced to leave nine items of luggage at the Victoria Hotel. These items were retrieved in November with the help of a courier.

Meanwhile, Joicey's son and daughter were still held in some comfort at a small spa called Bad Wildungen. The valet was not so fortunate and was sent to Ruhleben, a large prisoner of war camp near Berlin. As a condition of their safe return, Alfred and Joicey had committed themselves to rescuing those left behind and immediately began to write to Lord Balfour to ask for an exchange with Germans held in detention in Britain. Their attempts were at first refused by the government as published in The *Sheffield Daily Telegraph* for August 25, 1914:-

> We are officially authorised to state that the announcement made yesterday to the effect that Mr. Balfour on behalf of the Government will today meet Lord Joicey and Sir Alfred Haslam at the Foreign Office to discuss the question of an exchange of prisoners with Germany is absolutely devoid of foundation.

The government waivered and a list of names was drawn up. In a letter to Alfred written on September 1, Joicey wrote:-

> My Dear Sir Alfred. I am so sorry I am unable to be with you tonight - wired you to this effect this morning, asking you to add to the list for Mr Balfour the name of my daughter's 'maid' Kate Farley if it is not there already. I see by the papers there is some probability of exchange. I hope it is true. Kindly let me have a line after you have seen Mr. Balfour. If I can do any good, I could run up tomorrow if you will send me a wire.

A letter sent by Joicey on November 18 tells of his son and daughter's safe

return:-

> Dear Sir Alfred, Many thanks for your letter of the 14th inst and your kind congratulations with regard to the return of my son and daughter with their Doctor. My daughter managed extremely well to get them out of Germany, although she had great trouble and was once arrested as a spy, and I am very happy to be relieved from anxiety about them. Dr. Barty King said she managed splendidly and ought to go into the diplomatic service. He states they never could have got out without her

Over a year later Joicey wrote in a letter dated December 29, 1915:-

> My dear Sir Alfred, I have often wondered how you are getting on after our bad experiences in Germany & hope that you have now recovered from the effects, & that you & your family including your married daughter, are all well. Robin Fulton who was detained with my servant at Ruhleben only returned home last week as an invalid, but does not seem to have suffered much from his detention, as he was the most time left in his hotel…

However, he had not been able to rescue his valet from the internment camp at Ruhleben and in a letter of April 4, 1918, he wrote:-

> My valet poor fellow is still there, but I hear he is making good use of his time having learnt to write & speak fluently French & Spanish & become an expert in shorthand & type writing.

One member of that unfortunate party was T. W. Greene who later wrote of the happy times spent in Bad Homberg, reminiscing:- The time of year brings back the pleasant days spent among the people who were not then called Huns and Boche, when the agreeable parties from England used to meet.

# 16B

# The War Years 1914-1918: Hilda's Marriage

Shortly after their return from Germany, the marriage of Hilda Annie Haslam to Reverend Herbert Ham took place with all due celebration at Morley church rather than Breadsall Church which was closed due to recent fire.

The reception was held at Breadsall Priory, the guests numbering around 150. [*Derby Daily Telegraph* September 15, 1914] The birth of their two sons during the War was something to celebrate. Their first child, Christopher Haslam Dillon, was born in 1915 and died in 1994 (incapacitated in 1939) and Michael Jervase born in 1917 and died in 1941 unmarried. Herbert died 1965. Hilda predeceased her husband, dying in 1958.

> At the date of the wedding Reverend Ham was vicar of St James Church Derby, subsequently he became the Vicar of Wirksworth and then vicar at All Saints Church, Derby. After the church was made the Cathedral of the new diocese of Derby in 1927, he was appointed as the first Provost in 1931. He retired in 1938 to be priest in charge of Lee, Dethick and Holloway and died aged 95 in 1965.

**Lady Ann Haslam with her two soldier sons.
Left Eric, Right Kenneth.**

During the Great War Eric served with the Territorial Artillery (Captain) and was wounded at Loos in 1915. Then in 1916 he was injured in a railway accident in France. Subsequently he was placed on the Reserve List of Officers and employed in the war-work activities at the Company.

To help meet an urgent demand for munitions the Government asked for firms to undertake production. In late 1915 the Haslam factory was adapted to assist the war effort. A building was erected for production of shell cases. Alfred's nephew, Gerald Haigh Haslam (son of William G Haslam) had enlisted in the army but he was brought back to manage the shell shop. Previously he had been an engineer in the factory, designing and installing machinery. With so many men at the front there was the need for female workers to take their place. Gerald courted one of them, Gladys Finlay, and they were married in 1917.

The family's joy over the marriage was however overshadowed by the death of Alfred's son Kenneth in action. Kenneth had joined the Royal Field Artillery and gained the rank of Captain. Sadly, he was killed in action on April 27, 1917, at Guemappe and buried at Tilloy British Cemetery. Kenneth is also commemorated on the Trinity College War Memorial.

Subsequently, as a memorial to Kenneth, Sir Alfred commissioned a stained-glass window to be installed in the Lady Chapel of Breadsall Church. A dedication service was held on April 10, 1918, the ceremony being conducted by the Bishop of Derby. A report in the *Derby Daily Telegraph* [April 11, 1918] gives a full description of the window which has three lights. Along the bases of the three lights there is a memorial inscription to Kenneth.

During 1919, Sir Alfred offered to provide a sixth bell to the peal at Breadsall church; this was to be in memory of Kenneth. John Taylor's Bell Foundry, Loughborough were given the job. Their quotation, dated August 26 1919[9], reads:-

The total cost of supplying this bell, cast of the purest metals, perfect in tone, complete with fittings namely headstock, wheel, roller, clapper, crown staple, gudgeons, bearings etc., all of the latest type, including carriage of all materials and tools, and fixing the bell with its new fittings complete in the tower is £94 nett. Inscriptions, to order, are sixpence per letter.

The inscription on the bell reads:-

To the Glory of God
And in the Memory of
Captain William Kenneth Seale Haslam RFA
Who was killed in action in the Great War
In France on 27 April 1917
When rescuing his wounded comrades
Presented by Sir Alfred Seale Haslam, Breadsall Priory
`Easter 1920

A letter from the bell foundry dated October 25, 1919, states:- the bell will be a musical sixth above the present tenor (largest bell). Thus, with this tenor E the note of the bell will be D. Its weight will be between 4 and 4½ cwt.

His sister, Edith, donated her own memorial to her brother in the form of a silver book rest.

Many letters of condolence would have been received following Eric's death. One from James Horlick casts a little insight into their grief and the grief of others who had also lost a child on the battlefield. For example: -

September 21, 1918

Kidbrooke Park, Forest Row, Sussex.

Dear Sir A. Seale Haslam

My wife and I thank you so much for your kind letter of sympathy with us over with our terrible loss and we hope you will accept our sympathy with you on your terrible loss. You and I are very very proud of our sons who have made the Great Sacrifice but as you say it takes the sunshine out of our lives. I do hope your dear wounded son will be spared to you. We have to carry on to the end with this terrible war. My blow was very sudden. I had a cable from the War Office telephoned to me on the Tuesday saying he was terribly ill and next morning saying the worst had happened. You met him at Gairlock he was always so very cheerful. How is it you and I never met since our Gairlock days. Do look me up when you come to Town. We are are often at 2 Carlton House Terrace. My wife joins with me in kindest regards. Believe me. Yours very sincerely James Horlick

E H Vestey wrote on June 23, 1917 commiserating about the death of Kenneth

Just a line to express my sympathy in your latest trouble. I was very sorry to hear of it, goodness knows you have had your share - I am thankful to say our boys are alive up to the present, my boy has beeninvalided Home for past 6 months but now tells me he expects to go out again any day – it looks as though the war is going on for a long time yet – this Country is getting ready on a large scale & they are getting keener on it every week – It is not possible to realize it here as one does at Home – everything here is, on the surface, just as normal as before the War -

With the exception of Venezuela all our extensions are completed and we dont intend to start any large schemes now until we see how things look after the War. It appears to us the whole outlook calls for accumulating reserves rather than Plants - With kind regards. Yours sincerely, E. H. Vestey

> 'Vestey Brothers' firm was a long-time Haslam client. They were international dealers in the meat trade and pioneers in the use of refrigeration. They owned a fleet of refrigerated ships and were users of refrigeration installations and cold stores. They established cattle ranches in South America and Australia and became a large business.

A letter, March 31, 1915, written by an acquaintance Mr Durning-Lawrence is of interest. It was written after Eric had been initially injured but before Kenneth's death.

March 31, 1915

13, Carlton House Terrace, S.W.

Dear Sir Alfred It was a real pleasure to see your hand writing & to hear news of you all. Often have I thought, I will write to Lady Haslam & enquire how you all are, & then the absolutely necessary postponed the not absolutely necessary. I am very sorry to hear of Lady Haslam's illness. She is naturally anxious about everyone & everything & human strength will not go beyond a certain limit & then the wire bends if it does not break. The times become more and more difficult & more & more anxious. I find it so in my small way & I very often long for the strong hand to give advice & help. I hope however that Torquay will do much to restore Lady Haslam.

Eric has had a bad time altogether but you have him safe & that is something. Sir Ronald Ross is at present the head of a government commission to investigate malaria & other similar diseases & he wrote me a short time since that they that they hoped very shortly to return most of the men to the front cured – Kenneth has been fortunate so far.

I am here until Wednesday. We usually come up for a few days at the beginning of each month for business engagements - We were both extremely well all through the winter & then Dora had a sharp attack of Influenza taken I think from the soldiers at the Canteen & I took it from her in a similar form. She is quite well but I have not quite regained my strength. The weather continues so very trying & very serious for farming operations Three inches of snow this morning. Ascot is the Depot for the Flying Corps & the place simply swarms with them. Every empty house is crammed full of them & it is none too healthy. The tents however are being put up on the race course & as soon as the weather is fine the men will remove to them which will be much better.

Our Ascot doctor made me promise that Dora would not help again at the Canteen nor go to any place where there was a collection of soldiers. The Canteen has been closed because all the helpers were ill & there was no one left to help. We shall be here again the first week in May & then go to Bournemouth for a fortnight & then be here for about six weeks just to see old friends.

As well as the shell case production there are references, in letters dated 1918, to other war work activities at the factory:- a large volume of war work which has recently largely increased. And that the Government:- are sending a large quantity of machinery here to assist to double the output of guns, and to make matters worse they have pressed me to against my wishes to open up a factory in the town to turn out a large quantity of bombs which we are starting next week. With the date being a only few months before the Armistice most likely it never came into being.

Another blow followed swiftly after Eric's death when John, Alfred's eldest brother, died on May 14, 1917. The brothers had been close, though living miles apart. John had been one of the first students to attend Rawdon College in Yorkshire in 1859. On November 5, 1862 he was welcomed as pastor at Gildersome in Yorkshire where remained until 1893 when he became headmaster of Turton College, a preparatory school, which later became New College, Harrogate[39]. He had, like Alfred, a deep interest in history and was a member of the Baptist Historical Society. In 1912 he wrote a history of the Baptist Society of Yorkshire as the one most knowledgeable. He married twice and had several children - a son - William J Haslam.

In 1918, it was 50 years since the Haslam business had started in the Union foundry. Celebrations were in order but Alfred was barely up to it. A letter was received from the widow of Edmund Pontifex, a long-time associate of Alfred and one of the Directors of the original limited company.

December 18, 1918

Hill Crest, Bishops Waltham

Dear Sir Alfred, I was very sorry to hear from you that you had been indisposed and that you feel the strain of business too much for you. You have passed through such a terribly anxious time and the loss of your two sons must have been a great blow to you. Please accept my sincerest sympathy. Thank you for enclosing the slip of paper giving the particulars of your firms Jubilee. I found it most interesting. My husband always spoke of you as a Genius and I realise this after learning of the great things you have done. I was surprised to know I was the only outside shareholder but I feel whatever you do my interest will be quite safe with you. With kind regards, I am yours truly, M K. Pontifex

A letter from Sir Kenneth Anderson of the P & O Company, addressed from the Ministry of Shipping, St. James's Park commiserated with Alfred's state of mind and body in the immediate post war years:

May 1919

Dear Haslam,

It was good of you to write and I do infinitely appreciate your congratulations. What has happened to both of us leaves life an affair of dust & ashes except for friends & their good opinion which will always be precious. I'm sorry to hear you have been unwell, & wish you a speedy recovery. Iam hoping to return to my old haunts in the City soon & if ever you chance to come to London would appreciate a call if you can spare the time.

# 17B
# Philanthropy and Good Deeds

Sir Alfred's concern for the welfare of others was everywhere apparent. This came from a Christian ethic which extended beyond his own allegiance to the established Church.

His concern for the wellbeing of the Company's workforce is evident in several ways. In 1881 a Sick and Funeral Club was run at the Works, organised by William. He was liberal with gifts to retiring employees as in this instance. George Henry Handley of 35 Otter Street, a terraced house across the river from the foundry, was 70 years of age when he wrote this thank you letter in December 1918. He had been a foreman at the foundry, having settled in Derby from Lincolnshire.

> Sir Alfred, knowing your thoughtfulness for old servants of the Firm, I feel that your handsome gift to me is one more instance of your unfailing kindness and consideration. I respectfully tender my sincere thanks. Your gift is doubly welcome, it is a very practical help to me, and also brings the comforting thought that my services have been appreciated this also means a great deal to me.
>
> I trust that good health will wait upon you and yours for many years, and that the great reputation & prosperity of your Firm may be maintained. Believe me Sir Alfred, Yours faithfully George Henry Handley

He had an ecumenical regard for church and chapel alike. While he lived on Duffield Road, he and his family worshipped at All Saints church, now Derby Cathedral. He encouraged the vicar to carry out much needed repairs, donating £500 towards the restoration of the Church tower. He gave £100 towards new bells at St Peter's and £500 to new windows at St Werburgh's Church, Normanton. In Little Chester he financed a new aisle for St. Paul's church and a new school room for the Mansfield Street Methodist chapel.

He played a major part in setting up a Church Army Labour Home in 1891, when he was Mayor. Premises on Mansfield Road were found with rooms for ten beds, and Captain Billington, a Church Army evangelist and his wife, were placed in charge. It soon became overcrowded and the home moved to 9, Derwent Street, Derby. For many years he supported retired clergy through contributions to a Clerical Aid fund. Numerous donations were made to local causes; these included £100 to the new Infirmary. For two years he was President of the Derbyshire Hospital for Sick Children. Much valuable work was done under his personal supervision to place the Hospital in an excellent condition. An important project was his purchase of land at the rear of the hospital for future extensions.

An instance of his generosity comes in Rev Charles Kerry's History of Smalley. The Morley alms-houses, a seventeenth century endowment by Jacinth Sacheveral of Morley (1656), were situated almost at the entrance to Breadsall Priory. Reverend Kerry asked for, and obtained a photograph of these, a row of six attached cottages, three for the poor of Morley and three for Smalley. In acknowledging the source of the photograph, he wrote:

'It is only a last resource for those who prefer freedom to a home in the Union. One of the late inmates, a Smalley man, told the writer himself that, "Had it not been for the generosity of Sir Alfred Seale Haslam, M.P., of Breadsall Priory, he must have been starved to death." [40]

It is unlikely that the people of Derby were aware of many of Alfred's charitable acts but they are testified to in the letters of appreciation, the majority from organisations in London and the surrounding area. The letters show his deep interest in the welfare of children who were orphaned or from poorer families, and whom he assisted through gifts, customarily an order for the delivery of a sheep from the British and Argentine Meat Company.

It was a practical form of charity. From 1882 until his death, regular donations of a sheep were made to the Baptist 'Spurgeon's Orphan Homes' in London. Two or three times a year a sheep was donated to St John's Foundation School, Leatherhead, which had been founded for the education and maintenance of the sons of poor clergy, and to the Clergy Orphanage Corporation which maintained two schools, one in Canterbury for boys and another in Bushey for girls. In 1915, the 'Infant Orphan Asylum' sent him thanks for his *very welcome and useful gift'.*

The unmarried mother was also embraced: thanks for his *great kindness*es' were sent from 'The London Female Guardian Society', based in South Newington and founded in 1812 for the 'Rescue and Reclamation of Betrayed and Fallen Women'. Another grateful recipient was the *'Haven of Hope'*, founded in 1893, which soon became the *'Mission of Hope'* running nine hostels and homes for mothers and children in South London. They begged for additional assistance, to purchase meat at *'rock bottom prices'* direct from the shipping company and he was able to help them in this way.

The *'Friendless and Fallen'* was yet another charity he supported, not only with gifts of sheep, but also by sending tickets for an occasional treat. The value of a sheep was estimated in the books of the Clergy Orphanage Corporation at £3. Not in current times a large sum, but then would have been significant, particularly when repeated over many years and to many charities, it would have added up to a substantial amount. Bequests in his will were also made to charities.

# 18B

# The Art Collector

Alfred had a long-time love of art. By the 1890s, at his home 'North Lees' on Duffield Road he had filled the house with art works:-

> Sir Alfred has gathered around him an immense number of works of art and beauty, selected with the taste of the connoisseur, and the "household goods" at North Lees form a collection of whose possession any nobleman might be proud.

These art works would have been removed to Breadsall Priory. At the Priory Alfred had both the space and money to continue to indulge his love of art. He was always on the lookout for new works to adorn the walls of the Priory and in 1906 he commissioned three Minton wall plaques and a medallion from Marc-Louis-Emanuel Solon. The largest plaque, as suggested by Alfred's request for a procession, was entitled '*The Tribute to the King*'. Solon wrote:-

> The plaques are, I think, as good representation of my work as I have ever produced. I finished them with special care, and I hope you will be satisfied with the results.

Alfred was a noted collector of ivories. Recently (2019) two pieces of his collection have been placed in auction. These were not antiques but late nineteenth century depictions of medieval scenes. One piece that he once owned is a Dieppe ivory wager cup in the shape of a standing female figure whose skirts form a bell-shaped bowl, carved with a fifteenth century scene of the marriage of Maximilian I and Anne of Burgundy. Another, rather gruesome continental piece is a model of the Iron Maiden of Nuremburg, again a medieval scene, with hinged doors studded with ivory nails to close upon the part-naked maiden[41].

Alfred was fond of landscapes and sought out artists in this genre. He bought several paintings through the Vicars Brothers. One of the artists who attracted him was Albert Goodwin (1845-1932), a noted English landscape painter. He specialised in water colours which showed the influence of J. W. Turner and of the Pre-Raphaelite Brotherhood. Having seen one of his paintings in a London Gallery, Alfred sought him out, writing to his home in Bexhill, Sussex. The artist was slow to reply but ultimately several letters were exchanged, and in June 1917 he wrote:-

> My dear Sir
>
> Pray forgive my delay in the answer to your first letter. My somewhat lame excuse is that it came when I was away from home and was somewhat belated when it reached me; and then I was so fully occupied in making some "Artistic Hay while the sun shone". I put off the answer till I reached home when your second letter reminded me of the things that most of us have most to answer for sins of omission. I have several rather large drawings going on - most of them on the average about the size of 'Binares' (the drawing you speak of as having seen in the Pallmall Gallery). One of these is a Coast Sunset with a Stranded Ship. Another is Taormina Sicily. Another "The Ending of the Day". Mary Magdalen and the other Mary at the Sepulchre & for explanation I quote "But we trusted it had been he that should have

redeemed Israel". One or two other things I have going on within oil and water colour and a good smaller in water colour and oils. Perhaps you will be at some time in this neighbourhood when I should be delighted to show anything you like to see. Faithfully yours

November 12, 1917

My dear Sir,

I trust by now the Drawings chosen by you have reached you. Mr Martin Leggatt to whom I entrusted the Framing and sending off to you informing me a week ago that they had been dispatched and as you ask me to send account I now do so-

Patmos £30, Chichester £30, Pisgaly £18

I hope you will like them at least not less than you did when seen here. Thank you very much for asking me to pay you a visit in the spring. If I am alive I shall look forward to it though at my age life becomes as uncertain as death is certain but I am optimistic and look upon both as good and am content which any way they come home. For I have had (as Millais said in his last illness) "a very good innings". Trusting you are well and with kind regards

April 18

My dear Sir,

I am sorry to say I have no recollection of the crime you tell me of in your letter but I confess to a very bad memory and it may be possible that the letter you tell me received no answer was the one I do remember as holding. The suggestion that I should paint you an important Picture for the next RA:

If this is so the rather bad excuse for my not writing must have been in the fact that I put the matter off until I had something which I would call important on the Easel. But the thing did not arrive and so I suppose the letter that ought to have been written was forgotten. Pray forgive me for I quite acknowledge it must have seemed very wanting on my part.

I'm glad you like the "Sunset from a City wall" well enough to purchase it. It was begun two years ago and only completed just in time for...... humbly yours

As he became known as a collector of art, friends and dealers drew his attention to works he might be interested to buy, as illustrated by two letters from Thomas L Devitt of 13, Fenchurch Avenue in London. The subject matter is two paintings, one by Thomas Cooper, a landscape artist who specialised in rural scenes with cattle and sheep, and the other by Patrick Nasmyth (1787-1831), a Scottish landscape painter. From the tone of the letters Devitt and Alfred knew each other well:-

September 16, 1912

My dear Haslam,

I do not know whether you are back from Homberg or not, but I write to tell you that you must see the very best picture that Cooper ever painted as you ought to secure it. It is an upright picture which was exhibited in the 1851 Exhibition & was sold some years ago from a great Collection for about 900 gns. You can have it for £375. If you can put the picture which now hangs between the North & the East pictures within the dining room or Elsewhere this new one will make a noble addition to your Collection & will look splendid in the Billiard room -The picture is at Leggatts' in St James' street – The Manchester people were looking at it the other day & liked it much. Don't lose this, you decide against it – But I strongly advise you to have it – It will I beg you– If I could hang it I would certainly buy it myself. It is a good investment. Yours sincerely

January 5, 1914

My dear Haslam,

I am sorry I did not write soon after my very pleasant visit to Breadsall, but I was very tired at Christmas & not very well so I was lazy & spent a good deal of time in the holidays resting. I am very well now thanks for enquiries. I saw the picture by Patrick Nasmyth at Leggatts' & also their books showing that they paid £450 for it, then they sold it for £5000 to a client who soon after sold his house & some pictures – They gave him £450 for the picture & at this price offered it to you & me – I find that there are some American buyers who probably would buy it & as I am so much in love with the work I have secured it for a friend if hang splendidly on the oak panel at the right side of the billiard room window & it will be a joy to you & your friends. I believe Agnew got 900 guineas for it when he first sold it – It is as good or better than that one in the National Gallery & will always keep its present value I feel sure. Kindly write me by return if I am to have it sent to you or not. Love to all.  Yours sincerely

The Leggatt Brothers were London art dealers and picture framers. In 1920 Alfred visited their shop at 30, St James' Street and saw a painting by William Shayer (1787-1879), an English landscape and figure painter, which he subsequently bought.

September 4, 1920

Dear Sir. We beg to thank you very much for your letter and for kindly taking the Shayer picture, which we will keep awaiting your kind instructions. We will at once let you know of any good specimens we meet with and hope to do sosoon. We had a very good small picture by this artist which we sold only last week. We wish we had the opportunity of showing you. With our best thanks. We are Yours respectfully

Over the next three years Alfred sought contemporary art works through the Leggatt Brothers and another well-established London art dealer, the Vicars Brothers of 12, Old Bond Street who specialised in fine art printing.

June 3, 1921

Dear Sir Alfred,

According to our promise yesterday, we now send you particulars of the two pictures which you looked out and admired.

The picture by James Stark "Near Whittingham", outside measurement of frame 28" x 35"; size of picture itself 23" x 16"; price £375. (Three hundred and seventy-five pounds.) The William Shayer is entitled "On Dursley Common, Hants" and measures 25" x 24" outside of frame, and the picture itself is 16" x 23½". Price £180. (One hundred and eighty pounds.) The oil painting by Stark is a very fine specimen in his best period, and we strongly advise you to purchase this.

With regard to the Shayer, as we told you, it is under offer to a client who has been searching for a specimen by this artist for some time, and has promised to send his wife in to see it. If he does not decide to take it, we will give you the next refusal. Trusting to hear favourably from you. We are, Yours faithfully, Vicars Brothers

> James Stark R. A. (1794-1859) was a landscape painter, son of a Scottish artist, Michael Stark who settled in Norwich. James was influenced by Cromer and was a member of the Norwich School. William Shayer (1787-1879) was an English landscape and figure painter.

In 1911, Alfred bought a print from Vicars Brothers, perhaps showing a sentimental side to his nature. This was 'Lady Anne Culling Smith and children', engraved by Henry Scott Bridgwater (1864-1946) from a painting by John Hoppner R. A. Through them, in 1920 he bought an engraving of a similar subject, 'Beaming Eyes' engraved by Sidney E. Wilson. He also purchased two prints from painting by George Moreland, both engraved by Wilson. These were sporting prints, 'the Benevolent Sportsman' and 'The Sportsman's Return'. Alfred continued to buy prints rather than paintings.

December 28, 1921

> Dear Sir Alfred, we are pleased to inform you we have sent off this day per passenger train, your framed engraving of "Mrs. Sampson". It looks very nice indeed, and we trust you will like this engraving when you see it hung upon your walls. We would like to mention that in the Spring we are publishing a mezzotint engraving in colour of the famous picture by Gainsborough "The Blue Boy". Mr. Wilson is working on the plate at the present time, but as we announced our intention of issuing this engraving in the "Connoisseur" we have had so many applications for copies that we have very few left to sell.
>
> We do not wish any of our old clients to be left out, and although we are unable to send you an illustration at the moment, we should be glad to know if you wish us to reserve a copy on your behalf. We are afraid that the whole number will be subscribed for before we send out the usual notices. Wishing you the compliments of the Season

In 1917, Vicars brothers tempted him to him to buy a large 8ft.8ins. high x 7ft. wide painting by Alma-Tadema. Sir Lawrence Alma-Tadema (1837-1912) was of Dutch origin but settled in England in 1870 and his classical subject paintings, many of imaginary scenes of decadent Rome in the later years, were, and remain, very popular. There is no evidence that he bought it.

Sir David Murray, R. A. (1849-1933) was an eminent Scottish landscape painter who trained at the Glasgow School of Art and established himself in Marylebone, London in 1882. He became a full member of the Royal Academy of Art in 1905 and was knighted in 1918. His popular paintings, often with a romantic theme, are in the Royal Collection and hang in many Art Galleries and private homes. He and Alfred became friends. David Murray wrote to him:-

June 8, 1922

> 1, Langham Chambers, All Souls Place, Portland Place.
>
> My dear Sir Alfred, your reassuring first script regarding your eye-recovery was very pleasant to read & your pen work gave evidence that all is going well with you. I am in a whirl of social functions here just now I have just returned from a Whit holiday with friends at Wroxham but I cannot resist your kind invitation to see you in your home & your beautiful county, on Monday next the 12th I shall leave by some train about 2.15 arriving at Derby about 4.55 but shall see & send P.C. with exact train. My engagements here are rather crowded I shall only be able to remain a day or two. I dine with your friend Lord Southwark at his Company the Skinners on Thursday 15th & am wondering if by good luck you also are to be there. Very faithfully yours

## The Patry Portrait

One of the artists introduced to Alfred by the Leggatt Brothers was Edward Patry (1856-1940). Patry was born in Marylebone, London. He studied at Glasgow School of Art. Portraits were a speciality. Alfred was looking for someone to paint his portrait in older age. Patry took the commission and the portrait was painted. Alfred hoped to see it hung at the Royal Academy show in 1922 and it was initially accepted.

January 13, 1922

> Dear Sir, we beg to inform you that we have heard from the artist Mr. Edward Patry R.B.A. and he will be so very pleased to see you at his studio, 14a Kensington Crescent, on Tuesday next at 12 o'clock. It is a small house, approached from the road down a short drive, and we think quite easily found. With regard to the Nasmyth landscape we are reserving for your kind refusal /the outside size of the frame is 35½ inches long and 29½ high. With our best thanks, we are Yours respectfully

April 27, 1922

> Dear Sir, I much regretted to hear from Mr Patry at the beginning of this week that your portrait was crowded out for want of space. I need not say how disappointed he is and so am I for it is the worst luck a man can have for his work to be accepted and then no place found for it. It really is just a question of luck which makes me think more and more every year what a lottery it is. I have the portrait here again now and have replaced the glass keeping it safely until you are ready to receive it. Trusting you are experiencing benefit from the treatment to your eyes. With our best thanks. I am yours respectfully

The portrait of Alfred was returned to Derby and hung at Derby Museum and Art Gallery, not what Alfred had hoped for:-

October 28, 1922

> Dear Sir Alfred, I have just come across the enclosed photographs which you kindly brought for me to see before I began your portrait which I now return. We both so much enjoyed seeing your very interesting collection of pictures and your lovely old house. I wonder if you are coming to town this next week to see the Goodwins at Leggatts; many are very beautiful & have already found purchasers. The curator at Derby has sent me a catalogue of the Exhibition, it contains many good names & should be an interesting show. I am much obliged to you for allowing your portrait to be shown there & I much hope someone will be induced to follow your good example, and sit to me early in the new year.

The frame received some rough handling and was placed in the hands of Robert Ward whose Art Gallery was on Friar Gate. The frame was sent to London for remedial work while the painting stayed in Derby.

January 12, 1923

> Dear Sir, I wrote to Messrs Leggatt of London & quoted them for regilding the portrait frame now at the Art Gallery. I have received their reply asking me to pack the frame to London without the portrait & glass as they are asking the man who made the frame to put it right. Do you happen to have the case in which it travelled from London? Perhaps you would kindly let me know. Yours obediently R. Ward

February 2, 1923

> Dear Sir Alfred, I see from the printed form sent me from Derby that the Exhibition closes on the 7th Jan. I hope your portrait will be returned to you safely & I thank you again for allowing it to be exhibited there. With regard to my other work "The Least of These" as at present I have no room to show it in my London studio I would suggest your hanging it in your house for a few months; perhaps one of your friends might be tempted to purchase it, or if after living with it for a time you cared for it sufficiently to present it to Derby Art Gallery collection I would let you have it at a special reduced price, for it is a work I should much like to have it in a permanent collection but unfortunately I cannot afford to quite give it away.

> With regard to your portrait, if you wish it to be sent again to the R. Academy it might be as well to approach Sir David Murray & should his reply not be satisfactory, if you wish I would send it to Paris in February, this would however cost you about £6 - I should think.

> I often think of your charming Old Priory & the treasures it contains & hope you are keeping well & your sight is improving. With kind regards to Lady & Miss Haslam & yourself

Even David Murray could not help to reverse the decision not to hang the portrait and could only commiserate.

# 19B
# London Connections

Being a director of a company and having a knighthood meant Alfred had the status to qualify for membership of London gentleman's clubs. The citation for his Coat of Arms states that he was a member of The City of London Club, The Devonshire Club and The Reform Club.

Gentleman's clubs became increasingly popular during the late Victorian times. They were designed to allow members to relax and create friendships with fellow members. Meals and drinks were available along with overnight accommodation. These surroundings would have enabled Alfred to 'network' by exchanging information and developing professional and social contacts to help promote his business.

The Reform Club, which stands in Pall Mall, served as Sir Alfred's London home. He joined in April 1902 as '*Engineer and Director*' [proposed by Sir Arthur Sutherland and seconded by A E Leatham][15]. The Club had been founded by radicals as a response to the Tory Carlton Club but over time it became more generally liberal in its membership. The building was elegant and it was place where he could invite people to dine.

During the 1880s Alfred had connections with 'The Worshipful Company of Coachmakers and Coach Harness Makers'. In 1889 he was admitted by Redemption into the Freedom of the City of London in the 'Worshipful Company'. This was in recognition of his position and reputation in the commerce world, [*Redemption ie on payment of a fee*]. This rank led him to proceed to livery [*Senior membership*]. In 1904-05 he served as Master of the Company. This was accompanied by many banquets, and he hosted and funded an annual banquet. In 1906 he presented a silver Loving Cup and Cover to the Company[11], but was not able to attend the presentation, as seen by the letter below:-

A Court of Mayor and Aldermen holden in the Inner Chamber of the Guildhall of the City of *London*, on Tuesday, the 21st day of *September* 1889 and in the 53rd year of the reign of VICTORIA of the United Kingdom of Great Britain and *Ireland*, Queen, &c.

*Whitehead* Mayor.

THIS DAY Mr. Chamberlain having presented unto this Court *Alfred Searle Haslam* to be made free of this City,

IT IS ORDERED,

That the said *Alfred Seale Haslam* be admitted into the freedom of this City by Redemption in the Company of *Coachmakers and Coach Harness Makers*

*Monckton*

N.B. If this Order is not executed in Three months it will be void.

July 14, 1906

Dear Sir Seale, I duly read extracts from your recent letters to me at the Court on Thursday, and on your behalf, formally presented the Cup to the Master, who on receiving it, expressed himself as on the other side. The Cup was handed round and much admired, a resolution being passed to the effect that the presentation be duly recorded in the Court Room (in addition to that moved by the Master) both of which were unanimously received and with acclamation. The Cup attracted much attention at the Dinner, at which as well as at the Court, regret was expressed at your inability to be present. With regard to the past Masters' jewel this has never yet been really awarded, and I am therefore unable to send it to you. The invariable rule is that it is presented to the recipient in person, at the Court, upon formal resolution, and he is invested by the Master. I observe you do not anticipate being at the meetings still to be held this year, but no doubt, we shall have the pleasure of your company next January. Yours faithfully Thomas Henry Gardiner, clerk

Alfred was admitted, also by redemption, to the Merchant Taylors Company, one of the most ancient of London's Livery Companies. He became a free (an ordinary member) on February 18, 1897, and proceeded to livery (senior membership) only two weeks later on March 2, 1897. Apparently this was an accelerated promotion as most freemen had to wait several years before joining the Livery[12].

> *The **livery companies** of the <u>City of London</u>, currently 110 in number, comprise London's ancient and modern <u>trade associations</u> and <u>guilds</u>, almost all of which are styled the 'Worshipful Company of...' their respective craft, trade or profession. London's livery companies play a significant part in <u>City</u> life, not least by providing charitable-giving and networking opportunities. Liverymen retain voting rights for the senior civic offices, such as the <u>Lord Mayor</u>, <u>Sheriffs</u> and <u>City of London Corporation</u>, its ancient municipal authority with extensive local government powers.*

At times Alfred attended their dinners held in the Merchant Taylors' Hall. The Hall on Threadneedle Street, in the heart of London, is the City's oldest medieval banqueting hall, dating from 1347. Burnt out during the fire of London in 1666, and extensive damage by fire in 1940, parts of the building Sir Alfred would have known have survived. There is an impressive suite of rooms built around a courtyard, including a great hall, a parlour lined in carved oak panelling, a Court, and a library. Sir Alfred used the Hall for private functions He dined with friends and invited guests. These events would have provided 'networking' opportunities. From various letters sent in reply to invitations the dinners were very enjoyable:-

1905

I will be very pleased to be your guest at the Merchant Taylors' Hall on the 6th July & enclose a formal acceptance in terms of the card of invitation. It is quite a long time since we met & I shall be glad of the opportunity of seeing you again. I hope Lady Haslam & the young ladies are well. My kind regards to them. G.S. Yuill.

October 27, 1919

My dear Sir, I regret to have to inform you of the death of Sir Joseph Lawrence Bart J.P., D.L. a member of the Court of the Assistants of the Company, which took place on Friday the 24th instant in his 72nd year. Funeral service at Kenley Church, Surrey, tomorrow (Tuesday) the 28th instant at 2.15. Interment at Coulsdon Churchyard. A Memorial Service will be held at St. Margaret's, Westminster, on Wednesday the 29th inst,at 12.30 p. m. Yours faithfully, Thos Hy Gardiner

April 15, 1922 – handwritten

Dear Sir Seale, I read Miss Haslam's letter to the Court on the 12th inst. It was received with much regret, and I was instructed to assure you of the sympathy of your colleagues and their wishes for your speedy recovery, in which I entirely concur. Yours faithfully, Thos Hy Gardiner

Letters from Lismore, Heathside Road, Woking, Surrey – handwritten

April 13, 1913

Dear Sir Alfred. There has been a little delay in your note reaching me owing to my having recently changed my address But I hasten to say that I shall be very pleased to dine with you on Wednesday 7th prox at the Merchant Taylors Hall. Yours Sincerely Frank Ritchie

June 20, 1914

Dear Sir Alfred, Many thanks for your letter. We have had so little direct communication criticisms from our Stockholders that I fancy that there will be no hostile remarks at the meeting. Still one can never be certain and if you are likely to be in town, we should welcome you as one of our valued friends and supporters. Sincerely yours, Frank Ritchie

November 12, 1920

Dear Sir Alfred. Very many thanks for your kind thought of us. The pheasants arrived in good order & are much appreciated. We are enjoying the spell of fine weather though I fancy we get more fog in the mornings & evenings than you do. With kindest regards to Lady Haslam and yourself Yours Sincerely, Frank Ritchie

Letters from 2 Paper Buildings, Temple, London E.C

February 7

Dear Sir Alfred, I am delighted to dine at the Merchant Tailor's Hall on Wednesday Feb 22. Would you care to come to the Temple Church on Sunday the 26th & lunch with me at the Middle Temple Hall. Yours very sincerely, Butler Aspinall

Tuesday

Dear Sir Alfred, would you care to come to the Temple Church next Sunday the 29th, and afterwards lunch with the Middle Temple Benchers. If yes, I will meet you outside the Church after service. If I should miss, will you find your way to the Middle Temple hall & ask for me. Yours sincerely, Butler Aspinall

Tuesday

> Dear Sir Alfred, I enclose an Order for the Temple Church for Sunday the 6th May. I am delighted to dine with you the same evening at the Reform Club, 7.30. It will be a great pleasure to see you again after this long lapse of time. Yours very sincerely, Butler Aspinall

Five handwritten letters from the Admiralty, Ashley Gardens, London:

January 18, 1923

> Dear Sir Alfred, many thanks for the invitation to the Merchant Taylors dinner on the 31st inst. & I shall look forward to meeting you on that day. Sincerely yours R.B. Dixon

February 7, 1923

> Dear Sir Alfred, I have been trying for some days to write and thank you for the very pleasant evening I spent with you at the Merchant Taylors Hall last week. Until then I had no idea there were such palatial places in the City & I envy you in belonging to such an ancient Guild. Believe me, Sincerely yours, Robert B. Dixon

June 6, 1924

> Dear Sir Alfred, I very much regret that I am unable to accept your invitation for dinner at the Merchant Taylor's Hall on July 2nd as I have already accepted an invitation for that day at Lancaster House. I am particularly disappointed as I have such pleasant recollections of my last dinner in that Hall. Very sincerely yours, R. B, Dixon.

October 27, 1926 - typed

> Dear Sir Alfred, I have very much pleasure in accepting your kind invitation to dine with you at the Merchant Taylors' Hall on 10th November. Sincerely Yours R, B, Dixon

November 11, 1926

> My dear Sir Alfred, I am writing to again thank you for the most enjoyable evening I spent with you last night. I attend many dinners in town but none are more delightful than those given by the Merchant Taylors. I hope you feel none the worse for your visit to town?  Very sincerely yours, Robert B. Dixon

Alfred's son, Eric Seale Haslam, also joined the Merchant Taylor's Company by apprenticeship (Servitude) a means of entry involving no technical training. His Master was F M Fry who was Master of the Company in 1895 and 1911. Eric would have been 'apprenticed' at age 14-16 and was made 'free' (i.e. an ordinary member) on February 2, 1916, then gained livery a short time later on February 17, 1916[12].

# 20B
# Literary Connections

Most of the letters written from the Reform Club are from Henry William Wolff (1840-1931). He was the author of books and articles on co-operative banking and co-operative agriculture. From the correspondence it may be that Alfred invested money in him since in 1918 he enclosed the previous year's balance sheet with a letter. He wrote, '*Here is, together with my best wishes for the New Year, one Annual Balance Sheet, just to hand. I know that you like receiving it, so I send it at once, without myself having had a look at it.*'

There was a rapport between them which Wolff describes as '*boyish chaff*', alluding to Alfred's ownership of the Priory. Here are some examples:-

February 16, 1916

> Dear Haslam, when is that promised visit of the autocrat of Breadsall to his loyal metropolis coming off? You have announced yourself but not come. Let me know, please, when and if you do come. For I as a rule leave so early now, in order to be up at an unearthly hour, that without my knowledge of the coming of the venerable Prior I might be gone when that worthy personage puts in an appearance. Yours faithfully H. W. Wolfe

March 2, 1917

> Dear Haslam, here you are – to hand this morning. Let me have it back please, after digesting it. I hope you are thriving as usual. But I wish you would not send me your dark 'Unionist' weather. I suppose we shall be seeing you here shortly. It reassures one to see an old face……. amid this crowd of new members. The new batch about to be elected to the Committee includes Sir Jesse Boot and Sir R or A Winfrey. What a blessed thing suspension of the Ballot is. Yours sincerely, H. W. Wolfe

January 10, 1918

> Dear Haslam, you must not take so gloomy a look of things. It is natural that you feel down. Every other would in the same circumstances as is found. You know that under your guidance in matters requiring expert knowledge – I take precisely the same view of the Hull Cos Finances as yourself. However, the War, which costs us dear enough, in all countries is doing untold trouble to the world. There is so much to consider in this connection, the various counts are so many, it is hopeless to enter into detail but all round I see up, which probably could come up and the curds. I doubt Labour to almost absolute being it that is promised … Yours sincerely, H. W. Wolfe

Another literary acquaintance was Sir Edwin Durning-Lawrence (1837-1914). Born Edwin Lawrence, he added Durning to his name in 1898 in honour of his wife's maternal grandfather when he was created a baronet. His own father made a fortune in construction and two of his six elder brothers became Lord Mayors of London. Having trained as a barrister, Lawrence entered parliament as M.P. for Truro in 1895 as a Liberal Unionist. Alfred would have met him there in 1901.

He is best known for putting forward the idea that Sir Francis Bacon was the true author of Shakespeare's plays. He wrote books to popularise this and numerous books on other subjects. A major archive of his writings was donated to the University of London library in 1929[34].

His wife, Edith Jane Smith (1844-1929), whom he married in 1874, was the daughter of John Benjamin Smith. Their only child, a son died two days after birth so the barony became extinct at his death. With her niece Theodora {Dora) Edith was at Hilda's Haslam's wedding in 1914. Edith was an author in her own right. She wrote a family history of the Lawrence's of Cornwall and collected and published notes and illustrations on James Smith of Coventry (1731-1794)[34]. Their London home was 13, Carlton House Terrace, S.W. and their country home was at King's Ride, Ascot. There is only one short note from Sir Edwin but six letters from his wife Edith, only partially dated, reveal their friendship. The first is a response to a letter of sympathy sent on the death of Sir Edwin, written and posted in a black edged envelope on May 15, the year being illegible. Edith died of bronchitis and heart failure on April 27, 1929.

> 13, Carlton House Terrace,
>
> My dear Sir Alfred - You must excuse me for not having answered your very kind letter, but as you can believe there has been such an amount of business to attend to that time has failed me. Thank you & Lady Haslam so much for all your kind words of sympathy – It is a great joy to find how much my very dear one was loved & respected & I know how very much he will be missed.  He died just has he would have wished, full of work & interest to the last & then like a wounded bird he just fell from his perch. For me the separation cannot be very long but for Dora the loss is grievous – I am sorry to hear that you have been ill. <u>Do</u> take care & do not work too hard. I am sure Edwin worked much too hard for a man of his years & he was so very unhappy about the political world -Please give my love to Lady Haslam & to Hilda & Edith. Believe me Yours most sincerely Edith J. Durning-Lawrence
>
> 13, Carlton House Terrace, June 29
>
> Dear Sir Alfred I shall be very pleased to see you on Thursday but let it be 5 ok tea or dinner as otherwise you may not find me at home Mr & Mrs Whitham from Cambridge (she was a Holt) are coming to us this week. I congratulate you very much on Hilda's engagement if as I conclude it meets with your approval. To my mind the greatest possible happiness is to see ones children happily settled during ones lifetime. Someone has to be fit & by the order of nature it should be the old ones. Yrs very sincerely Edith J. Durning-Lawrence

## The Bemrose Library

In 1908 William Bemrose died. He was the second of three sons born to William Bemrose, the founder of Derby's most important printing company and he became a director of the firm. He was also a director of Royal Crown Derby Porcelain Works and a notable collector of porcelain on which he wrote several works. He also collected art works and wrote and published a major biography of artist Joseph Wright of Derby as well as other works, including a manual on wood carving. He died at the age of 77 leaving a rich legacy. His home was Elmhust in Lonsdale Place, Derby, which he filled to the brim with collections.

His porcelain collection went into auction but he also had a library of rare quality: 5,000 books, 300 volumes of pamphlets, newspapers, portraits, charters and deeds etc. In September 1911 George Nathaniel Curzon wrote to a number of people in Derbyshire to gain their financial support for his proposal to acquire the library for public use. Amongst people to receive a letter was Alfred:-

> Dear Sir Alfred Haslam You may perhaps have seen in the … of Friday about the effort I am making to secure the Bemrose Library of Derbyshire books etc for the County or Borough. It is a point with which I am sure you will be in sympathy. My father & I have started the sub with £100 each & the Duke of Devonshire, Herbert Strutt, Mrs W Evans & Sir H Raphael have each given similar sums. Very shortly I am going …… a public appeal in the Press but I thought I would write to you in advance in case you might be willing to join us. I shall be very glad if this is the case.

Alfred contributed £25. On October 3, 1913, a public appeal was published in the *Derbyshire Advertiser*[35]. Curzon was successful in raising the money and the library now forms an important part of Derby Local Studies Library collection.

# 21B

# Business and Competition

By the 1890s a great number of cold air machines were operating worldwide on marine and land installations. However, they were losing ground due to competition from other types of machines that were more economical in operation. These used a refrigeration system which required ammonia or carbonic acid (carbon dioxide) as refrigerants. Originally these types were not acceptable for marine use. Over the years, firms had introduced improvements and during the 1890s these machines had been successfully used to preserve shipments of frozen goods in addition to land-based installations.

To compete with other firms, Haslam's developed these types of machines in preference to the cold air types. By 1910, a range of machines had been developed including new patents. Trading continued profitably, the 1923 catalogue claiming that 3,100 machines were in use around the world for a variety of cooling and refrigeration purposes totalling 23. Examples given included cooling of chocolate and food products; storage of hops; freezing of meat, fish and rabbits; drying of photographic plates and grain.

At an Extraordinary General Meeting in 1891 a resolution was passed that company shares should be offered firstly for purchase by family members rather than the public. It was also agreed that the minimum number of Directors should be reduced from three to two. In 1908, the firm was converted from a public limited company into a private limited one. By then company shares were owned by Haslam family members with one exception. This being Edmund Pontifex a long-time associate of Alfred and one of the directors of the original company, by this date he had retired and appeared on the share register as a *'gentleman'*. Edmund died in 1909 and his shares were passed to his wife Margaret Kate Pontifex.

By far the greatest number of shares was held by Sir Alfred. The new company rules required a minimum of two directors; these were Alfred and his brother William Gilbert. [*National Archive records*]

# 22B
# Troubled Years

**Lady Ann Haslam**

On March 11, 1924, Alfred's wife, Lady Ann Haslam died. She was described as of quiet disposition who devoted her life to family matters and running the household. She supported Alfred, *with much charm and success*, in carrying out his public duties. Her burial took place on March 14 at Morley Church following a ceremony at Breadsall Priory led by the Bishop of Derby, at which the family and a number of estate tenants were present.

At the Priory a local organist played a selection of Lady Haslam's favourite church music. A motor hearse and vehicles conveyed the coffin and mourners to Morley Churchyard where the coffin was carried by six estate employees to the grave *'lined with snowdrops and evergreens'.* As well as Sir Alfred and family members a large number of friends gathered in the churchyard for the committal service[42].

After Ann's death Alfred made a will leaving most of his estate to his children, Eric, Hilda and Edith. Sir Alfred died less than three years later, aged 83, on January 13, 1927, at St Pancras Hotel London, while on a business trip. The funeral followed five days later. On Tuesday January 18, it was reported in the local paper as follows:-

SIR ALFRED SEALE HASLAM

> The late Sir Alfred Seale Haslam was laid to rest in Morley Churchyard yesterday. Early in the day a private service for relatives had been held at Breadsall Priory, the residence of the deceased conducted by the Bishop of Derby. The deceased's works and foundry at Derby were closed and members of the staff at the works acted as pall bearers. The coffin was borne by tenants and employees of the estate. Over 300 employees of the firm attended.

Particulars of the Alfred's will were published in the local press:-

> The whole estate amounted to an estimated £1,064,39s.7d. Estate duty already paid £288,000.8s.4d. The executors of the Will dated 12 April 1924, after the death of his wife, were Captain Eric Haslam, Mr William Haslam JP, and Col. Godfrey Mosley[43]. The Breadsall Priory estate and property at Morley were left to Eric and a number of houses on the Duffield Road were settled upon Hilda and Edith. The bulk of Sir Alfred's collection of china and other articles were left to Eric, whilst most of the pictures are divided among the children.

> A sum of £100,000 was settled on Eric who also receives £50,000 absolutely; £75,000 was settled on Hilda and a similar sum on Edith, each of them to receive £25,000 absolutely; £50,000 is settled on Sir Alfred's grandson, Ronald Victor Haslam. Legacies of £1,000 were to be paid within a month of death and free of duty to each child, and £500 to Mrs Victor Haslam, the testator's daughter in law. Mrs Victor Haslam receives an

annuity of £800 per annum, and there is an annuity of £200 per annum to Mrs Buckley. Another annuity of £150 was left to his cousin Miss Smith. Pecuniary legacies went to The Rev. Canon Ham £5,000; William E. Haslam £10,000; Gerald H. Haslam £3,000; Frank I.R. Tatam £1.000; A. V. Hough £1,000. Legacies to charities (A total of 18 charities that received either £100 or £200 legacies were listed in the press article. These were local and non- local organisations).

The residue is given by way of augmentation to the funds settled on the children and Mr Ronald V Haslam pro rata and to be added to portions held in trust.

Tuesday April 5, 1927

Additional details of the will Sir Alfred Haslam, of Breadsall Priory, were published to-day. He left £500 in trust for his butler, Herbert Keene, for life, and then for his children; £200 to Frederick John Newham, chauffeur, if still in his service; and £50 each to his other servants and farm hands who have been with him for three years. He gave £1,200 in trust to the Rectors of Breadsall and Morley Churches to distribute to the poor of the parishes on his birthday October 27.

On his death, since Sir Alfred was the principal shareholder, the Company had to be sold to enable his estate to be administered. Other properties including houses in Chester Green were also sold.

# 23B

# Eric and Edith - Breadsall Priory

When Sir Alfred died in 1927, his surviving son, Eric Seale Haslam, inherited the Priory. He lived there with his sister Edith Hannah. Edith, born 1882, did not marry. She was well known, throughout the County, as a supporter of charitable projects. In 1927 she founded a hostel for working girls at St Christopher's Home for Wayfaring Women in North Street, Derby and later on another at St Michael's House, Osmaston Road. For many years she was on the management committee of the Queen Victoria Memorial Home of Rest in Derby, Chairman of the Breadsall Branch of the Red Cross and one of the managers of Breadsall School.

**Edith Haslam**

She later wrote a book, *The Garden of Two Keys*, published by Oxford University Press. It was in the form of weekly letters, originally written to her god-daughter, June. The little girl had been so delighted that Edith thought other children might appreciate them.

Around 1930 she promoted the idea of turning the old graveyard of St Alkmund's into a *garden of rest and children's playground*. After much legal work a faculty to proceed was granted. Edith undertook to donate the whole of the money for fitting out the area together with an endowment for a caretaker and future maintenance. A trust was formed and five trustees appointed to manage the funds. Edith was invited to open the 'St Alkmund's Garden' at a formal ceremony on August 31, 1932. That evening it was reported the area was crowded with children along with mothers chatting or knitting and watching the children at play.

One interest that brother and sister shared was the gardens, which were later enhanced with a programme of tree planting. A visitor to the Priory in 1938 wrote of the - *air of comfortable well-being...... the well-kept lawns and gardens...... everything's in harmony.*

A columnist of the *Derby Daily Telegraph* in June 1932 reported:-

> I went over to Breadsall Priory and, after tea with Miss Edith Haslam, Mr Eric Haslam her brother, and Sister Ward of the St Christopher's Home for Wayfaring Women, was taken to look at the terrace, rock garden and stream. There are some grounds which never give a caller the pleasure occasioned by the first visit, but those belonging to Breadsall priory have the knack of making a greater appeal every time they are seen. A flag path had to be treated carefully because of the aubrietias which grew in every crevice. In every shade of purple, they were exquisite. On being advised to look the way I had come, one of the prettiest garden pictures met the gaze. Flowers, bushes and trees hugged the line of the rivulet and, in the distance, a flame coloured azalea added just the right touch.

Both Edith and Eric lavished attention on the gardens which were regularly opened in aid of charity. For example, in June 1935, a notice in the local paper announced:-

> Captain Eric Haslam, brother-in-law of the Provost of Derby, is opening the gardens of Breadsall Priory to-day in aid of the Derby Cathedral Organ Fund. The grounds will be open from 2.30 to 8 p.m., at a charge of 6d, cars 1 shilling. Miss Haslam is arranging to have tea served in the Priory at a charge of 2 shilling per person.

During the year 1937-38 Eric was appointed as the High Sheriff of Derbyshire. In August 1937 the local paper reported:-

> An enjoyable time was spent by members 230 Battery, Old Comrades' Association, and their wives at garden party in the grounds Breadsall Priory, as the guests of Mr. E. S. Haslam, High Sheriff of Derbyshire, who was a captain of the Battery. Mr Haslam and, his sister Miss Edith Haslam, acted as hosts. During the afternoon the party visited the different parts of the estate, the Priory Farm, and the ornamental and kitchen gardens. Bowls, quoits, clock golf and darts were also played. Tea was taken in a marquee on the lawn, and an entertainment and community singing followed. Mr. F. Dunham, the assistant secretary, thanked Mr. and Miss Haslam for their hospitality, and congratulated Mr. Haslam his appointment High Sheriff and County magistrate. He also commented on his continued interest in his old Battery. Major S C Wright, who was the Battery commander, seconded this. There were 80 in the party, and the arrangements were made by Mr. J. Lowe, the secretary.

Edith died in 1941. Her funeral took place on December 30 at Morley Church.

In November 1943, Eric Haslam married Norah Apphia Woodroffe. Eric died, aged 61, in December 1967. His widow continued living at the Priory for a few years before moving to a new house built near the entrance lodge and lived there before moving to Oxford to be near her niece until her death in 1988. They had no children. Norah was a great benefactor to Morley Church and a long-time member of the PCC. The altar silver, at Morley Church, made by John Blackburn of Derby, is dedicated to Eric and Norah Haslam.

The priory was unoccupied and in 1970 the estate was put up for sale. It was bought by Charles Harpur-Crewe, whose family already owned much of the land around it. In 1974 it was leased to a local developer for conversion to a country house hotel and golf complex. Since then, under several owners, the priory and the estate has been further developed. It is Grade II listed and currently, 2020, is a 'Marriot' country house hotel and country club.

# 24B

# In Memory

## Morley and Breadsall Churches

Memorials dedicated to the Haslam family are at St Matthew's Church, Morley and, All Saint's Church, Breadsall. The churches are each around two miles from Breadsall Priory, the home of Sir Alfred's family.

**Haslam Grave, Morley Church**

At Morley there is a Haslam family grave for Sir Alfred; Lady Ann; Son - Alfred Victor; Son - Captain Eric Seale; Daughter - Edith Hannah. The ashes of Eric's wife Norah Apphia were interred in the grave. As mentioned previously the altar silver is dedicated to Eric and his wife Norah.

**Morley Church Window dedicated to William Kenneth Haslam**

At Morley Church, there are memorial windows in memory of Alfred's eldest son Victor and his third son Captain William Kenneth. William Kenneth was killed in action in France during April 1917 in 'The Great War'. In addition, at Breadsall, as described in Chapter 16B, Sir Alfred commissioned a window dedicated to William Kenneth together with a sixth bell to the peal, which was inscribed in his memory.

## St Mary on the Bridge Chapel, Derby

**Bridge Chapel. 1954 view**

The Bridge Chapel is one of the few chapels of its age remaining in the country and has records that date back to the beginning of the fourteenth Century. It stands beside the eighteenth century St Mary's Bridge, which replaced a medieval bridge, across the River Derwent. In 1912 the chapel was closed and allowed to deteriorate so that by the 1920s it was in a ruinous state.

In March 1928, at the AGM of the Derbyshire Archaeological Society, the chairman announced that, being the Jubilee year, it was fitting to celebrate it with an outstanding event. A chance had come to acquire and restore the chapel.

The owner, a Mr Walley, had died and the chapel had come on the market and through the promptness of Major Briggs the chapel was secured for £750. *(applause)*. The meeting agreed to support the plans for the restoration which was estimated to cost £2,000. As well as the chapel the purchase included the adjoining house and a small amount of land fronting the river. A funding appeal was to be launched.

In February 1929, at a meeting of the Society the chairman disclosed that – a person whose name must for the time remain anonymous had offered to pay for the restoration of the chapel and the adjoining house as a memorial to a family relative. When asked to whom the memorial was to be dedicated, he replied 'a family relative and one who bore a very honoured name in the county of Derbyshire'. A formal proposal to accept the offer was adopted. The appeal mentioned above had raised £750, this was to be included in the funding[43, 44].

Subsequently it was revealed that the benefactors were Eric Haslam and his sisters Hilda and Edith in memory of their father Sir Alfred. Restoration was carried out in 1930 under the direction of local architects Percy Currey and Charles Thompson, in close cooperation with the Society for the Protection of Ancient Buildings. A memorial in the chapel reads:-

Giving thanks to God
For the long life and work of Alfred Seale Haslam
Knight of Derby and Breadsall Priory
Eric - Hilda – Edith- His children repaired this ancient chapel
St. Mary on the Bridge.

# Overall Observations

Alfred's early working life, during the 1860s, coincided with a period in which, refrigeration systems were being developed. Also, nationally, there was the need to increase the meat supply to feed the increasing population.

Surplus meat in the form of mutton and beef existed abroad for example in Australia. Consequently, there was commercial interest in methods by which meat carcases could be exported to Britain. Ships fitted with refrigeration systems for storing frozen carcases would enable this to take place.

Alfred possessed a 'go-getting' spirit. At the age of 24, he persuaded his father to purchase the Union Foundry to set up business together as a general engineering company. Subsequently, a limited Company was formed in 1876, with Alfred, aged 32, as managing director.

Knowledge and experience of refrigeration systems, must have been gained early on in the company's life as only five years later, by 1881, cargos of frozen meat had been successfully transported from Australia to Britain on ships fitted with 'Haslam' refrigeration machinery. Over the years the business rapidly expanded, refrigeration machinery being supplied internationally for marine and land installations for a diversity of applications. During this time the factory was extended, in stages, to cover several acres and became a major employer.

Alfred took interest in the welfare of his workforce. For example, he provided an Institute for their recreation and houses of good standard. A Workers Sick Fund was established and in letters there are references to donations for retiring and sick employees. He invited the workforce and wives to celebrate family events. These included the 21st birthday of his eldest son Victor and later the newly married Victor and his wife. On becoming Mayor of Derby, he held a grand banquet for all his staff. Also, he was a regular patron of various charitable organisations, both locally and elsewhere in Britain.

Alfred was very active in politics, locally and nationally. During his time as mayor in 1890-91 he was knighted by Queen Victoria and later became an MP for Newcastle-on-Lyme for 6 years. These activities would have meant he spent periods away from the factory in his constituency and London etc. No doubt, during formal and social occasions he would have promoted capabilities of the Company and its products.

From early in the Company's life Alfred's 'right hand man' was his brother - William Gilbert Haslam - who as a co-director was responsible for efficiently managing the works and production. During Alfred's absences from the Company he would have been in overall charge of the Company. At the previously mentioned Mayor's banquet he was enthusiastically acknowledged by the workforce.

Married life for Alfred lasted 50 years, his wife Ann dying in 1924. They had three daughters and three sons. The profitable company enabled Alfred and his family enjoy a prosperous life style. Sadly, one of the daughters, Sybil, died when only one year old.

All three of the sons were employed in the factory. Tragedy occurred when the eldest son Victor died in 1907 leaving a wife and child. He was being groomed to succeed his father to take charge of the factory so it must have been harrowing times. Another distressing event was the death of another son, William, who was killed in action during WW1, aged 25. The remaining son Eric married but had no children. His two sisters Edith and Hilda died in 1941 and 1958. Hence, when Eric died in 1967, Alfred's branch of the Haslam family expired.

There is evidence in Haslam letters that during the 1900s Alfred was trying to sell the Company but with no success. However, in 1927, on the death of Alfred the Company had to be sold to settle death duties etc. Under subsequent owners the factory traded for another 10 years. It then closed with activities being removed to Scotland, thus ending the 70-year life of a business that had gained international standing.

Alfred's life can be summarised by this extract from his obituary published by *Derby Daily Telegraph*:-

> In the death of Sir Alfred Haslam, the town of Derby loses one of the greatest citizens it has ever produced. The great business which he built up affected life in every continent. It revolutionised stock breeding in the newer worlds and increased the standard of living in crowded cities and industrial communities of a large part of Europe, He commenced to revolutionise economic conditions by the introduction of refrigerating machinery. We have lost in him a great citizen of a town he loved and served so well.

----****----

# Appendices Part A

A. Early Day Experiments, *The Brisbane Courier*, December 12, 1925
B. Arrival of the Orient - *Western Morning News* October 4, 1881
C. Arrival of the Garonne - *London Daily News* and *Derby Daily Telegraph* October 25, 1881
D. Haslam Letters
E. Letter from Mr Ward of J & E Hall Ltd
F. Minutes of Meetings Re - Sale of the Company
G. Examples of Financial Accounts

## A. Early Day Experiments

This information is from an article in an Australian newspaper - 'The Brisbane Courier', December 12, 1925. It describes, in retrospect, early efforts in Queensland to establish the frozen meat trade; the author being a Mr T F Fauset. He mentions the 'Haslam Foundry and Engineering Company' and states that- *The first production machine made by the Haslam Co, my partner Mr W T Clarke and I brought out from England with us in the SS Merkara, the first steamer to inaugurate the direct mail service between London and Brisbane-leaving London on February 12 1881. Two months later the late Mr. Coxon left London for New Zealand with the second production machine.*

The machine was to provide freezing capability for meat at a new freezing works operated by The Queensport Meat Export Co Ltd. Mr. Fauset describes arriving at the site around April 1881. Apparently, he and his partner were supervising engineers for the site.

Then - *Early in July we had a run with the machinery and being anxious to have the credit of freezing the first meat in Queensland, the butcher brought me a sheep carcase. This I put in the chilling room for two days then moved it to the freezing chamber for some time. ...... I cut a leg off, which I hung for two or three days to defrost...... This was cooked for a Sunday lunch. So was the first meat to be frozen and cooked in Queensland.*

Later on, Mr Fauset and his partner were instructed to go to Sydney to inspect and test the freezing machinery in the steamers 'Garonne', 'Orient' and a chartered German liner 'Catania'. Machinery had been installed in Britain but no time had been available for trials before the scheduled sailing dates.

It was imperative that, if there were any doubts about efficiency, they were not to allow the ships to be loaded with meat as there was no insurance on frozen meat, and if not landed in good condition the loss would fall on the consignees. The machines were run for some time with no problems. It was decided that the ships could be loaded. The three cargos indeed arrived in London in good condition.

Mr Fauset and Mr Clarke were partners of an engineering firm. Mr Clarke in a letter to the paper, dated May 1884, refuting criticisms of the performance of Haslam Machinery signed himself as *Colonial Representative for the Haslam Foundry and Engineering Company Ltd.* Mr F Coxon referred to above with the second machine was a Consultant Engineer representing Haslam in New Zealand. He installed the machine at a new freezing works at Burnside in New Zealand. The official opening was reported in the *'Otaga Times'* dated August 5, 1882.

# B. Arrival of 'The Orient'

*Western Morning News* Tuesday, October 4, 1881:

By the arrival of the mail steamship Orient at Plymouth yesterday, the possibility of importing fresh meat from Australia into England has been illustrated and the experiment is likely to have an effect on the English meat market.

About a month since the Orient Line mail steamer 'Cuzco', arrived from Sydney with the first consignment of meat on a large scale from that distant colony, although the experiment had previously been tried in other of the Company's vessels to a smaller extent, in each case the results were so satisfactory.

Now three of the steamers on the Australian line are fitted with refrigerating apparatus for the conveyance of meat – the 'Cuzco', with the Bell-Coleman dry air refrigerator; and the 'Orient' and the 'Garonne' with the refrigerating machinery of the 'Haslam Foundry and Engineering Company Ltd', Derby.

On the arrival of the 'Orient' in Plymouth she was met by Mr Haslam, one of the patentees of the apparatus. The 'Orient' only had the apparatus fitted in her prior to her last outward journey.

The Haslam machines are made in various sizes and will deliver pure dry air – refrigerating (*the condenser*) with water at 90 degrees F – at from 40-60 degrees F below zero direct from the machine. (*Cooling*) Water and air enter the machine and refrigerator* at 90F. The air is compressed to about 40lb per square inch, and temperature to about 280 degrees F. It is then passed through the refrigerator* and then expanded, leaving the machine at a temperature ranging from 30-60 degees below zero.  One of the chief features of the machine is the production of pure dry air.  A second important feature is that the same degree of cold can be obtained as water at the refrigerator (*the condenser*) at 90F, as can be obtained with water at 50F. This is a matter of considerable importance when ships are passing through the tropics as the water available for refrigerating * ranges in the sea from 80-90F.

The Haslam machines are made in various sizes to deliver from 7,000 to 60,000 cubic feet of air per hour, and with an engine power of 70hp a cargo space capable of holding 250 tons of fresh meat or fish kept in a continually frozen state from Australia to England, and meat can be imported in a fresh and marketable condition.

The Orient brings from Melbourne 150 tons of meat comprising 3,161 carcasses of sheep, and a small quantity of beef. The whole of this was supplied by the 'Melbourne Frozen Meat Export Company' and was stored in the main and after hold. At Sydney the 'Orient' also took on board from the 'Orange Slaughtering Company' 180 carcasses of sheep and 122 quarters of beef besides a quantity of dead fowls and ducks required for use on the homeward voyage, these were stored in a separate chamber from the bulk of the meat.

On the voyage home the refrigerating apparatus, which adjoins the engine room, was kept at work 20 out of the 24 hours daily, except during the passage through the Suez Canal, when it was in operation the whole of the 24 hours.  The effect of the refrigerators is to freeze the carcases into hard blocks, incapable of impression until they have been exposed for some hours in an ordinary temperature, when they thaw, and present a precisely similar appearance to, and are said to be, as fresh and marketable, as sheep just slaughtered.

In Plymouth Sound that part of the refrigerator known as the snow box was reducing the temperature down from 60 to 80F below zero.  Intensely cold air was passing in a constant current through small trunks into the chambers containing the frozen meat. The temperature in these chambers varied from 10 degree F on the floor to 21 degree F near the roof.

On the homeward voyage the ship's steward has been constantly using the frozen meat for the passengers and crew. He states that it is perfectly sweet and wholesome. The full flavour of the meat is retained, and the officers of the Orient speak of the experiment as an unquestionable success. Twice a day during the voyage home Mr Scott, the engineer, made examinations of the chambers containing the bulk of the meat which is intended for the London markets. He reports on the working of the refrigerator in the most satisfactory terms, remarking that the carcases when put into the market will be equal to English mutton.

Judging from the excellent character of the meat and poultry consumed on the voyage the experiment is accepted by those on board as a success. This, moreover, receiving consideration from the fact that on her outward voyage she took with her 30 tons of fresh fish and meat for consumption. The action of the refrigerators upon the provisions was highly satisfactory, and the steward bringing back to England, as evidence of efficiency of the machine, a small portion of the fish in as wholesome condition as the day upon which it was first received on board.

The result of experiment in the case of ocean steamers carrying large numbers of passengers and crew is of the greatest importance. The apparatus occupies very little room, and can be affixed to any steamship. In this way the carrying of a large quantity of livestock on the upper deck may be avoided, whilst passengers will at the same time be assured of an adequate supply of fresh meat, poultry, and provisions.

The general effect of the introduction of meat into the country by such means opens up a very wide field for contemplation and speculation, in which the interest of the English cattle breeder and the English market are involved. The Company represented by Mr Haslam are already fitting up a large vessel for the sole purpose of engaging in the Australian meat trade, and the success of the experiment may result in the development of another means of competition with the home producer.

* Cooling of the air

# C. Arrival of 'The Garonne'

*Daily News* and *Derby Daily Telegraph* Tuesday, October 25, 1881:

The Orient Line mail steamer 'Garonne' (Captain Hillkirk) from Sydney August 31, Melbourne Sept 8 and Adelaide Sept 9 arrived in Plymouth Sound late on Sunday night and was boarded this morning. She is fitted with Haslam's dry-air refrigerator patented by the Haslam Foundry and Engineering Company, Derby, and brings 4,788 carcases of sheep frozen and preserved by means of the refrigerating apparatus.

The carcases are stowed in a main and second chamber, a third chamber being reserved for the stowage of frozen meat for consumption during the voyage. The carcases, weighing about 150 tons were embarked by the Orient Slaughtering Company at Sydney, the same company that sent the last consignment on the 'Orient'.

The refrigerating machinery fitted to the 'Garonne' is of the same size as that on board the 'Orient' but occupies a much larger space. The machinery was fitted at Birkenhead on the occasion of the vessel undergoing repairs, and under the circumstances more time and attention were devoted to the fitting than in the case of the 'Orient', where the apparatus was rather hurriedly fixed.

On the voyage out the 'Garonne' took about 30 tons of fresh salmon and various other fish, and this consignment is reported as discharged in splendid condition.

She also took out sufficient fresh meat and other provisions for the consumption of the passengers and crew during the whole voyage, thus dispensing with the carriage of the large quantity of poultry and livestock which hitherto encumbered the decks of ocean going passenger ships. In this respect the experiment was also most successful, the meat served up for consumption being in excellent condition.

On the homeward voyage there have daily inspections of the refrigerating chambers at intervals of two hours by Mr Kelly Chief Engineer and his assistants. In the tropics the machine was driven continually. Since leaving the tropics, however, it was only necessary to keep it going half time and 15 degrees F was the average temperature in the chambers over the entire voyage. In the Tropics the condenser cooling water was at 90 degrees F, but as with the 'Orient,' not the slightest difficulty was experienced in keeping the thermometer down to 50 degrees F.

It was found during the voyage that it was only necessary to keep the engine going sufficiently long to produce a temperature at from 18 to 20 degrees F in the refrigerating chambers, but according to the chief engineer of the Garonne not the slightest difficulty would be found in reducing the temperature down to 5 degrees.

This morning, when the 'Garonne' was boarded in Plymouth Sound the chambers were entered and inspected and the carcases were found to be in splendid condition. Immediately inside the door of the first chamber the thermometer registered 24degF but this spot was the least cold throughout the whole of the chambers.

The 'Garonne' had experienced heavy weather in the Bay of Biscay, and had rolled heavily. Consequently, the carcases had become disarranged and had fallen one on top of the other, where they had frozen together.

In the large chamber were several thermometers the lowest registering 15 deg. In some parts of the chamber where the moisture had congealed the deck was covered with snow to a depth of 5 or 6 inches. Ice crystals were overhanging overhead in many instances several inches in length and the appearance of the chamber was most picturesque. This was 6.30 in the morning and the apparatus had not been at work since four o' clock. The thermometer was 62 degrees on the upper deck and 70 degree in the lower deck cabins. The condition of the cargo is everything that can be desired. The machinery worked admirably, and the Chief Engineer expressed his entire satisfaction with it.

There were 130 passengers on board and they and the crew were regularly fed with the refrigerated meat, the saloon passengers being similarly provided. Not the slightest discoloration was discernible, nor was any other fault detected. All on board expressed themselves thoroughly pleased with the condition of the meat.

The 'Garonne' left the Sound early in the day for London where her cargo will be disposed of.

NB This paragraph was added by the *Derby Daily Telegraph*

The success of the experiment opens out the prospect of the meat supply of this country being very largely increased and consequently cheapened. Mr Haslam is to be congratulated upon the satisfactory application his patent which appears to have come out of a severe test in a manner which augurs well for its general adoption by the Australian Steamship companies.

# D. Haslam Letters

A few letters survive written to Alfred from his Father viz:-

### March 12, 1867

Envelope addressed:
Mr A. Seal Haslam,
Engineer at Messrs. Allsopps
Burton on Trent

Dear Alfred,
I think you are doing pretty well at Burton having comfortable lodgings and means of improvement in the evenings which you may not have in a new place. Still if you mind to move be sure and behave with honour, take no advantage what you sow you may expect to reap. I am not surprised that you should look out for improvement, but as you have had a good place, show some gratitude by behaving well at leaving.

I don't know anything respecting Sir W, Armstrong or his Engineer, but if you join them I hope you will find them honourable men. But in this matter as in all others make it a matter of prayer, ask for divine guidance. We are short sighted, and know not what a day may bring forth - without God's blessing we cannot be safe for a moment, we cannot prosper; I hope you will seek for, and enjoy this blessing and guidance, you will need it more than ever as years roll on, and as you are exposed to new temptations.

Yours affectionately

W. Haslam

P.S. You did not say anything about Annie we hope you have seen her at Barton or Burton We are sorry the weather is so unfortunate for country rambles. Give our love to her and all.

### Derby, April 3, 1867

Dear Alfred.

We were much pleased to receive your letter it did not get here by Morning post, which disappointed us. Mother began to think some evil had befallen you by road or rail we are thankful that God has protected you. You say difficulties presented themselves on every hand and side. We were sorry to hear that, but it gave us much pleasure to find they did not stop your progress.

Perhaps you will give us a few details of these obstacles, and let us know what sort of folks you are thrown amongst by this change. We were glad to hear that you got a comfortable room. Is there a good Mechanics Institution? or reading room? near you They have a very good one at the Sunday School Union and an excellent library, but perhaps that is too far off 56, Old Bailey London EC If you can I should like you to join them for 1 Quarter The expense is light, and they have great variety of reading all the best newspapers &c.

I am very busy and have not time for more in fact it is to you we must look for news, you must send three letters to our one, and let them be long ones as London is a wonderful place you have much to describe and send particulars about, especially about Sir W. Armstrong's works and progress.

Yours affectionately W. Haslam

PS I don't know whether the address you have given us be correct Penton Terrace I cannot find it London Postal Guide. I shall send a Derby paper if there be anything particular before long

### Derby April 6, 1867

Dear Alfred

I am glad to hear that my cousin is getting on in the world and shall be glad to hear all about his progress. I was rather taken by surprise when you expressed a wish to leave Armstrong's so soon as I thought it a first class place for improvement, still money is an object to a young man who would like to be in business by & by Mr Milward and yourself will be better able to judge than I can, whether you are likely to obtain the place if you apply; and to give satisfaction if you get it - you may of course depend upon the influence of myself and friends if it be needed, but I hope your own fitness for the place will do more than my influence, or I should not advise you to try for it - you speak of a letter to Mr. Bass I think that would be premature until you have made matters right with Mr. Canning:- if he approves of you I think all the rest will be easy. Let me know how you succeed with him. I send Mr. Bass's address below, but I should not advise you to call upon him without the consent of Mr. Canning. Your letter to John we send on to Atherstone, as they are now at Mr. Wiln's. Annie will write and give you all the news.

Mr. T. Bass Esq, 19 Lower Belgrave St, Baton Square, London

Affectionately yours WH

### Derby May 12, 1868

Dear Alfred,

I have been thinking you are not acting very kindly towards me. It is a long time since I had a letter from you. You are aware that my time has been fully occupied since my return from London making up lost time. - but I have got the younger members to write to you more than once or twice. I thought that would do quite as good as writing myself as I had nothing personal to communicate, but I much wished to hear how you were going on and where employed; and at what kind of work. How Mr Milward is, and what prospects for the future.

I send you advertisements of the sale of premises and Foundry late "Fox brothers". The Foundry is a good opening for anyone who thoroughly understands the business, but I do not think tool making at Derby has been a very good trade of late some years ago it was a first class affair, but other towns of late taken the lead I think Foxes were behind the times, and the great flatness of trade has given the finishing stroke, and perhaps there has been a want of economy. - if you were ready to begin the foundry seems a good choice that is if you had a knowledge of the details of the business, but I fear it would be too great and too speculative an undertaking under present circumstances.

You must not be surprised if you see Uncle Rowland next week I expect he will be called up to give evidence by the Derby Board of Health as to the fouling of the waters at Eaton which are sent down to Derby by the Water Company - if he comes he will stay at the Salisbury Hotel, Salisbury Square Fleet Street - but we will try to let you know exactly the time and place.

Yours affectionately W. Haslam

# E. Letter from Mr. Ward of J & E Hall Ltd. 1923.

HJW/MSB.

10. S.T SWITHIN'S LANE,
LONDON, E.C.

20th July 1923.

Dear Sir Alfred,

I have discussed with my colleagues the figures
which our Accountants, Messrs. Cooper Brothers & Co.,
obtained from Messrs. Watson Sowter & Co. last week.

As I mentioned to you when we last met we have been
asked by our financial friends to give them our opinion
on the question of a purchase based upon our providing
the management and we have necessarily to consider the
question as to how the two establishments should be
run so as to obtain the best results for both, economicall
and otherwise. The Accountant's figures for the past
nine years are of course important but we have to have
regard to the future even more carefully than the
past and I think you will agree with me that the period
which includes the war and post-war boom is altogether
abnormal while the re-valuation made in 1920 must
necessarily to a large extent be discounted by present
trade conditions. We do not feel that we can make
any recommendation to our friends until we have had an
opportunity of seeing the Works and this would entail
your giving us full opportunity for ascertaining
their condition and capacity. This means that we
would have to ask you to give us your full confidence
which I venture to think we may fairly claim and I
may say that for our part we would be glad to reciprocate
any courtesy you may see fit to extend to us by
inviting you to visit our Works at Dartford.

As some of my colleagues will be going on
their holidays at the end of this month it would
be a convenience to us to have your reply within
the next few days otherwise the matter had perhaps
better stand over until September .

I remain,

Yours very truly,

Sir Alfred Seale Haslam,
Breadsall Priory,
Near Derby.

## F. Minutes of Meetings Re-Sale of the Company in 1927

The following are extracts from minutes recorded in a ledger covering the years 1915 to 1927[11].

### a. February 15, 1927

**After the death of Sir Alfred.**

> Extraordinary General Meeting of Shareholders of Company held at Union Foundry. Derby on February 15ᵗ 1927.
>
> Present.
> Mr. W. G. Haslam
> Mrs L. M Haslam
> Mr E.S. Haslam
> Mr G.H Haslam.
>
> Mr. W.G Haslam was elected Chairman of Meeting.
>
> _____
>
> The Secretary read the notice signed by five Shareholders convening the meeting for purpose of considering, + if thought fit of passing resolution below, the meeting being convened by signatories in pursuance of powers conferred upon them by section 67 Companies (Consolidation) act 1908.
>
> The resolution that Mr. Eric Seale Haslam be appointed a Director of the Company for remainder of Year ending on 31ᵗ March 1927 was duly carried
>
> _____
>
> The Meeting before closing desired to place on record their regret at the loss the Company had sustained by the death of Sir Alfred Seale Haslam, Managing Director from its commencement, and to express their appreciation of the eminent services rendered by him to the Company for over fifty Years.
>
> M. G. Haslam.

**b. March 18, 1927**

**Sale of Company's Investments.**

Meeting of Directors of Company held at
Union Foundry, Derby on March 18ᵗ 1927.

Present
Mr. W.G. Haslam.                    Chairman
Mr. C.S. Haslam.

Minutes of meeting held February 21ˢᵗ 1927
were read, approved & signed.

It was resolved that Company's Investments
as per Balance sheet be sold & proceeds paid to
special account at Westminster Bank, Corn-market
Derby for benefit of Shareholders on register
at this date subject to claim, if any, for
arrears of Taxation. Alternatively if terms of
interest offered by Union Disct. Co. of London Ltd.
be more favorable, portion of proceeds to be lodged
with them.
The sale to be effected by —

| | | | |
|---|---|---|---|
| Westminster Bank Ltd. | £42.000 | 5% | War Loan |
| Coates, Son & Co London | £60.000 | 3% | Local . |
| Tenney & McGeoge, Glasgow. | £61.000 | 3½% | Conv. . |
| Stevenson & Barns, Derby | £25.000 | 5½% | Treasury Bonds |
| do. | £8.300 | 5% | N.Z. Loan. |
| do | £5.000 | 6% | Pref Union CS Co. |
| do | £1.000 | 4½% | Deb.    do |
| do | £18.000 | 4% | Funding Loan |
| do | 5 | | Old Shares Ind Coope. |

W.G. Haslam .

Chairman!

**c. June 14, 1927**

**Proposal for sale of Company approved by Directors.**

Meeting of Directors held at Union Foundry
Derby on June 14ᵗ 1927.

Present.
Mr. W. G. Haslam        Chairman
Mr. E. S. Haslam.

Minutes of Meeting held March 31ˢᵗ 1927
were read, approved & signed.

It was resolved & ordered that an interim
dividend of 6¼% less be paid this date
on account of Y.E. March 31ˢᵗ 1927.

Letter dated June 13ᵗ 1927 from Messrs Taylor
Simpson & Mosley having been read as to the
terms agreed for the sale of the Company and
its assets to Mr H.B. Potter it was resolved
same be approved and the Secretary was
instructed to arrange with them as to the
calling of necessary meetings of the Company
to elect Mr Potter a Director and to place the
Company in Voluntary Liquidation at such
dates and times as were required. The Secretary
was also authorized to sign any necessary
Agreement for and on behalf of the Company.

Mr. W. G. Haslam stated he had arranged to
sell ten ordinary shares to Mr H.B. Potter
and the transfer was approved

W. G. Haslam.
20/7/27
Chairman

**d. July 19, 1927**

**Agreement for sale approved.**

Meeting of Directors of Company held at Meadsall Priory. Derby on July 19ᵗʰ 1927

Present.
  Mr. W. G. Haslam    Chairman
  Mr C. S. Haslam.

Minutes of Meeting held June 14ᵗʰ 1927 were read, approved & signed.

Agreement for sale of Company to Henry Bland Potter & Jesse Lord was approved, and Common seal of Company was affixed in presence of two Directors named above & the Secretary.

Certificate for ten shares Nos. 178, 179, 379, 380, & 389 to 394 inclusive in favor of Henry Bland Potter was sealed & signed by two Directors & Secretary.

W. G. Haslam.
15/8/27

Chairman.

**e. October 13, 1927**

**Shareholders agreed to Company sale and voluntary liquidation.**

Extraordinary General Meeting of Shareholders of Company held at 35 St. Mary's Gate, Derby on Thursday October 13th 1927 at 11 a.m.

Present
Mr. W. G. Haslam
Mr. C. S. Haslam            } Directors.
Mr. Potter
Col. Mosley, as an Executor of Sir Alfred Seale Haslam

Mr. W. G. Haslam was appointed Chairman

The Secretary read the notice convening the meeting.

Minutes of Extraordinary Meeting held July 4th 1927 were read, approved & signed.

On proposition of Mr. W. G. Haslam seconded by Col. Mosley, it was resolved that the business be sold & disposed of to Henry Bland Potter and Jesse Howarth Lord upon the terms of an agreement dated the 25th day of July 1927 and expressed to be made between the Company of the one part and the said Henry Bland Potter and Jesse Howarth Lord of the other part, and that the Directors' action in entering into same is hereby ratified and confirmed.            Carried unanimously

Mr. W. G. Haslam proposed, Mr. C. S. Haslam seconded - that the Company be wound up voluntarily under the provisions of the Companies (Consolidation) Acts 1904 to 1917 and that Mr. Harry Carlyle Waddington of Trafalgar House, Waterloo Place, Pall Mall, S.W., Incorporated Accountant, be hereby appointed Liquidator

for purpose of such winding up and with power to carry out the sale of the Company's business agreed to be made to Messrs Henry Bland Potter and Jesse Howarth Lord and to execute all documents necessary to effect the same. It was resolved same be passed.

The date of confirmatory meeting to be fixed by Directors & notices issued to Shareholders at a later date.

W. G. Haslam .

# G.1. Comparison of Profit & Loss Accounts
## Years Ending March 31, 1877 and 1901

### Expenditure £

| Year Ending March 31 | 1877 | 1901 |
|---|---|---|
| Work in Progress (brought forward) | | 24927 |
| Stock in Hand (brought forward) | | 7405 |
| Materials/ Purchases | 8422 | 46789 |
| Coal and Coke | 732 | 2171 |
| Carriage | 810 | 1645 |
| General Expenses | 602 | 735 |
| Horse Keep and Hire | 193 | 173 |
| Rates and Taxes/gas/water | 90 | 1614 |
| Stationery | 122 | 304 |
| Stores | 375 | 761 |
| Bank Charges | 144 | 177 |
| Incidental Exp | 63 | 150 |
| Insurance | 24 | 135 |
| Rent paid | 700 | |
| Wages | 7323 | 31251 |
| Salaries | 750 | 6917 |
| Travel expenses | 84 | 417 |
| Loan interest | 189 | |
| Discounts paid | 24 | |
| Depreciation/plant/tools/stock | 244 | 1807 |
| Royalties | | 2995 |
| Charities | | 47 |
| Commission | | 196 |
| Agency & London Office Expense | | 550 |
| Legal charges | | 1258 |
| Advertising | | 745 |
| Bad debts | | 5663 |
| Totals | 20891 | 138832 |

### Income £

| Year Ending March 31 | 1877 | 1901 |
|---|---|---|
| Sales | 16299 | 124960 |
| Rent received | 70 | 106 |
| Plant made by Company | 976 | |
| Loose Tools and stock | 2544 | 8175 |
| Work in Progress | 1515 | 16408 |
| Discounts and allowances received | | 20 |
| Investment interest | | 1111 |
| Totals | 21404 | 150780 |

### Summary

| Year | 1877 | 1901 |
|---|---|---|
| Income | 21404 | 150780 |
| Expenditure | 20891 | 138832 |
| Profit £ | 513 | 11948 |

# G.2. Comparison of Balance Sheets
## Years Ending March 31: –1877 and 1901

### Liabilities £

| Year Ending March 31 | 1877 | 1901 |
|---|---|---|
| Share capital | 12880 | 47260 |
| Loans Mr Barton | 1300 | |
| Loans Mr Haslam | 3500 | 15287 |
| Sundry debts | 5116 | |
| Bank balance | 1553 | 15547 |
| Cheques presented | 115 | |
| Reserve Fund | | 616 |
| Workman's Insurance Fund | | |
| | **24464** | **78710** |

### Assets £

| Year Ending March 31 | 1877 | 1901 |
|---|---|---|
| Fixed plant and Machinery less depreciation | 10428 | 20128 |
| Tools and stock less depreciation | 8793 | 12878 |
| Valuing and legal | 439 | |
| Cottage Rents | 2 | 11 |
| Work in Progress | 1515 | 16408 |
| Debts owing | 3782 | 23558 |
| Cash in hand | 18 | 5512 |
| Freehold | | 25203 |
| Bank | | 23641 |
| Derby Cold Storage | | 5951 |
| Investments | | 14196 |
| Patterns /Drawings | | 2000 |
| | **24977** | **149486** |

### Summary

| Year | 1877 | 1901 |
|---|---|---|
| Assets | 24977 | 149486 |
| Liabilities | 24464 | 78710 |
| Surplus | 513 | 70776 |

166

# References Part A

1. Part of a Chinese verse offered to their Goddess of Cold in the Shih Ching - or 'food poems' c. 1100 BC. … *In the days of the second month, they hew out the ice…… in the third month they convey it to the ice houses which they open in those of the fourth…*

2. Old Testament, Job Chapter 38 verse 22: - *Have you entered the storehouses of the snow or seen the storehouses of the hail?*

3. '*Ice and Icehouses through the Ages*' by Monica Ellis.

4. '*The Meat Trade in Britain 1840-1914*' by Richard Perren, 1978.

5. '*A History of the Frozen Meat Trade*'. Also, *Dundee Courier*, January 25, 1881.

6. '*River Plate Fresh Meat Company*' Prospectus- *St James Gazette*, June 3, 1882.

7. '*A City Within A City*' by Joan D'Arcy.

8. *Effects of the Great War on Businesses - Sheffield Telegraph* December 31, 1914.

9. Emails with Alan Brown at Farnborough Air Sciences Trust (FAST) and Geoffrey Cooper- a retired Ministry of Works engineer.

10. Email correspondence with Schools and College, deleted.

11. Haslam papers plus Minute Book (1915 to 1927) and Account Ledger (1876 to 1901).

12. *Haslam and Newton Prospectus – Yorkshire Post* and *Leeds Intelligence*, October 24, 1928.

13. Grace's Guide.

14. Workman's Banquet - December 20, 1890 (*Derby Daily Telegraph* December 22).

15. British History on Line: The West India Docks.

16. Haslam Foundry & Eng Co Ltd - National Archive Ref BT31/30895/11055 (Researched by John Steeds).

# References Part B

1.   Birth register.
2.   1841 and 1851 census returns.
3.   Emails with Repton School.
4.   M. Tranter, ed., *The Derbyshire Returns to the 1851 Religious Census,* 1994, pp, 12, 72. The census recorded 50,000 Anglicans, 33,000 Methodists, 20,000 Primitive Methodists but only 6,000 General Baptists.
5.   S. Greasley, *The Baptists of Derbyshire 1650-1914*, 2007, pp94-107.
6.   *Derby Mercury*, September 1854.
7.   Rawsdon, Gilderson.
8.   Railway Apprenticeship.
9.   Family Papers.
10.  Emails with Trinity College.
11.  http://www.coachmakers.co.uk/history/show/pagename/gifts
12.  Email correspondence with Merchant Taylor Company's Archivist.
13.  John's letter.
14.  *London Gazette*, January 11, 1873.
15.  Emails with Reform Club.
16.  The house is no longer there.
17.  Permanent Record of Queen Victoria's State Visit to Derby, 1891, p140.
18.  Wright, *Directory*, 1874 gives no 34 but no 35 the 1881 census.
19.  *Derby Evening Telegraph*, December 22, 1890.
20.  *Derby Daily Telegraph*, June 23, 1914.
21.  The evening was reported in detail by the *Derby Daily Telegraph.*
22.  V. M. Leveaux, The History of the Derbyshire General Infirmary 1810-1894, Scarthin Books, 1999.
23.  Permanent Record of Queen Victoria's State Visit to Derby, p9.
24.  DLSL Building plan 4472 March 10, 1890, by Naylor and Sale. 2 villas for A. S. Haslam of North Lees. Frederick Road on the north side and facing Duffield Road.
25.  DLSL Building plan 5759 March 4, 1895, by Messrs Coulthurst & Booty, 4 villas for Sir A. S. Haslam of North Lees. East side of Duffield Road, below North Lees. Naylor and Sale, 2 villas for A. S. Haslam of North Lees. Frederick Road on the north side and facing Duffield Road.
26.  DAJ, *Codnor Castle and its Ancient Owners*, 1892, vol 14, pp. 16-33.
27.  P. H. Currey, 'Breadsall Priory', DAJ 27 (1905) pp127-137; J C Cox, '*The History of Breadsall Priory*' from documents with two stone artefacts photographed by Alfred Victor, *DAJ* 27 (1905) pp138-149.
28.  *Derby Daily Telegraph*, March 5, 1907.
29.  *Derbyshire Advertiser and Journal*, May 10,1907.
30.  National Portrait Gallery.
31.  Auction report. Amongst his many books was one published in 1891 written by William Lecky, *Liberty and Democracy.*
32.  *The Belfast News-Letter*, November 25, 1902.
33.  *Nottingham Evening Post*, November 6, 1903.
34.  Sir Edwin's collection of books and papers was bequeathed to the University of London as the Durning Lawrence library.
35.  There is a copy of the appeal in DLSL [BAO27.4; Bemrose library of Derbyshire books: important letter from Lord Curzon: an appeal to Derbyshire: reprinted from the *Derbyshire Advertiser* October 3, 1913]. An additional letter in the DLSL lists the names of those who contributed before the publication of the appeal in the *DA*, October 7, 1913. The list of contributors includes Sir Alfred's name set against the sum of £25.
36.  Deleted.
37.  *Derby Daily Telegraph* August 24, 1914.
38.  *Derbyshire Advertiser* June, 26, 1914.
39.  *Baptist Magazine and Literary Review*, vol. 54. p780.
40.  *DAJ*, vol. 1, p55, photo p. 54. M.P. dates this to 1901-1906.
41.  Kirk and Mellors auction website, September 2018.
42.  *Derby Daily Telegraph*, March 14, 1924.
43.  *Derby Daily Telegraph*, Saturday, March 19, 1927.
44.  *Derbyshire Advertiser*, April 6, 1928 and February 29, 1929.

# Information Sources

'*A City Within A City*' by Joan D'Arcy.

'*A History of the Frozen Meat Trade*' - by James Critchell and Joseph Raymond, 1912 - online.

'*An Illustrated History of Breadsall Priory*' by Nick Redman.

Australian & New Zealand Newspaper Archives - online.

British Newspaper Archives – online.

Christchurch City Libraries NZ.

Derby Local Studies Library (DLSL).

Derby Museums.

Derbyshire Records Office (DRO).

Farnborough Air Services Trust (FAST).

Grace's Guide.

Haslam Family Papers.

'*Ice and Icehouses through the Ages*' by Monica Ellis.

Library and Archive Service, London School of Hygiene & Tropical Medicine.

Little Chester Heritage Centre Archives - Chester Green Derby.

'*Modern Mayors of Derby*', 1835 to 1905 - *Derbyshire Advertiser*.

Permanent Record of Queen Victoria's State Visit to Derby, 1891.

Picture the Past Derbyshire - online.

'*Refrigeration Cold Storage & Ice–Making*' by A J Wallis Taylor, 1902 - online.

'*The Friargate Line*' by Mark Higginson.

'*The Meat Trade in Britain 1840-1914*' by Richard Perren, 1978.

Various web sites.

'*World Below Zero*' by Alan J Cooper.

A Commissioned Publication Printed by

MOORLEYS
Print, Design & Publishing
info@moorleys.co.uk · www.moorleys.co.uk